# CHRONIC MARKETER

Brad Gosse

Copyright © 2012 Brad Gosse

All rights reserved.

ISBN: 1470158647
ISBN-13: 978-1470158644

# TABLE OF CONTENTS

| Chapter | | Page |
|---|---|---|
| 1 | About Me | 7 |
| 2 | Why I Smoke | 27 |
| 3 | It's Never Been Easier To Own A Business | 31 |
| 4 | Who's In Your Corner? | 37 |
| 5 | Don't Let Fear Dictate | 43 |
| 6 | The Value Of Your Ideas | 51 |
| 7 | Creating Intangibles | 55 |
| 8 | White Label And Private Label | 65 |
| 9 | Don't Let Your Ego Dictate Pricing | 71 |
| 10 | Writing Sales Copy | 75 |
| 11 | Website Traffic | 93 |
| 12 | Webinars | 99 |
| 13 | Social Media | 105 |
| 14 | Blogging | 111 |
| 15 | Search Engine Optimization | 115 |
| 16 | Embrace Your Laziness | 119 |
| 17 | The 3 Phases Of Entrepreneurship | 131 |
| 18 | Outsourcing And Hiring | 135 |
| 19 | Not Caring What People Think | 141 |
| 20 | Productivity | 153 |
| 21 | Personal Branding | 165 |

## TABLE OF CONTENTS

| Chapter | | Page |
|---|---|---|
| 22 | You Are Not Scalable Your Content Is | 177 |
| 23 | Train People To Deal With You | 183 |
| 24 | Dealing With Assholes | 189 |
| 25 | Watch Out For Social Media Hippies | 195 |
| 26 | Analysis Paralysis | 199 |
| 27 | The Grass Is Never Greener | 205 |
| 28 | Don't Be Afraid To Ask For Money | 211 |
| 29 | Chamber Of Commerce & Other Assoc. | 217 |
| 30 | Changing The Rules To Your Advantage | 223 |
| 31 | Stop Watching TV | 229 |
| 32 | Dropping Out Of School | 235 |
|  | Acknowledgments | 241 |

# Chapter 1: About Me

So, what do you do for a living?

This is one of the hardest questions I have to answer. I used to just tell people "I'm in the porn business".

But that's just not true anymore. I can tell people that "I'm an Internet marketer". But that just makes me sound like a douche bag.

For the most part, I tell people I'm a software developer. It usually kills the need for follow-up questions which is just perfect for me, because I try not to define myself around my occupation if at all possible.

The reality is, I do whatever makes me money for the least amount of work. I'm not too fussy about what those things are as long as they are legal, easy, and allow me to sit on my ass and smoke pot.

For me it all started in the late 1990s. I was working in my dad's retail furniture store and running a part-time database consulting business. I've always been a bit of a computer geek.

But let me back up for a second. I never did well in school. In fact I failed as early as the sixth grade. Deep down it felt like I was just being lazy. I had no interest in public school. Nobody could explain why I had to learn certain subjects so I ignored them. Not necessarily the wisest move but I didn't know any better.

I did so poorly in school and got into so much trouble that I was kicked out and asked to spend seventh-grade at a different school. By the time everyone was applying for high school my principal told me I had no other choice but to enter a trade school. That's where people go to learn basket weaving and cake making. Everyone made fun of those kids.

I thought I had no choice. On the day when the teacher handed out enrollment forms for the regular high school I decided to take one and complete it. Later that day the principal had me fill out the forms for the trade school. When I think back now I realize that he had no real power but decided he was going to mess with the rest of my life.

All summer long, I thought I was going to have to go to trade school. That is until mid-August when I received my paperwork from both schools. Of course I was not there for attendance at basket weaving ;-)

High school for me was never to be completed. I spent a few years there mainly learning photography and how to manipulate girls. I left at 17 because I wanted to live on my own. It's very difficult to have an apartment and go to high school.

**Out On My Own**

My first job was working in a telemarketing office. Picture a telemarketing office in 1990. Long cheap office tables each containing 4 telephones, 4 index card boxes of leads, 4 notepads, 4 pens and 4 ashtrays. We were in the middle of a recession. Jobs were scarce especially for someone like me. So

I smiled, dialed and sucked back a pack of cigarettes every shift.

For some reason I wound up being very good at this job. The turnover was ridiculous, only a few regulars. These were veteran telemarketers. There was the carny, the Goth kid, the alcoholic, the weekend AM radio jazz DJ, and a few other stragglers. Somehow I was able to outsell the majority of these misfits.

We didn't sell anything so to speak. Instead we solicited donations for charities. The way I understood how the deal worked was this. A charity needed to make their budget for the year. Let's say they were short $1 million. Our company would write them a check in exchange for the rights to raise funds on their behalf with an unlimited ceiling. The charity got their budget shortfall and our company could raise as much as it wanted in return.

I learned early on that when you get people on the phone who are committed to a cause, it's just as easy to ask them for a few hundred dollars, or even $1000, as it is to ask for $10. While the majority of the people making calls would get a commitment for a donation and ask for $10, I would ask for $500. By the time I got down to $50 or $100 people would feel compelled to say yes. I was being lazy. I wanted to meet my quota in the minimum amount of calls.

My boss called me into his office. He told me if I could keep doing the kinds of numbers I had been doing I would be "taken care of". I was young, that sounded pretty good.

Before I knew it I was in his chair, managing people and teaching them to sell like me. I was 18 years old, getting decent sized paychecks and only working a handful of hours each day. This was awesome.

I started managing the day time room that called for corporate donations and discovered something funny. Call a pizza place and ask them to cough up money for a charity, almost all will say no. Back that up with a request for a free pizza and they all say yes. We had companies sending us designer hair products, rental cars, food and more, all to offer to our "fund raisers" as incentives.

It didn't take long before I got sick of managing telemarketers. With high turnover you also get a lot of legal hassles. My job was to often deflect these hassles.

When my dad called to tell me that his furniture store was booming and that he needed my help, I wasn't quite ready. However, after some convincing and a little guilt, I decided to quit being a telemarketing manager and start selling, delivering, and repairing furniture.

I will never forget uttering the words "all I want is a job that lets me sit on my ass and smoke pot while I work."

## The Porn Biz

It didn't happen overnight, but it did happen. Partially because I envisioned it. I'm not going to say that the universe delivered it to me in some hokey world where we wish for things hard enough and they happen. That's bullshit.

Six months after declaring what I wanted out of life, I built my first porn website. And with the first two hours of work invested I made $528.

That's when I knew, I needed to shift gears and focus 100% of my time on this project.

The first people to go were my database consulting clients who I had been working with on the side. I hated them. A week earlier a project manager dragged me into her office to scrutinize every hour of my previous month's invoice, and asked for concessions, a certain amount of time spent for free guaranteeing work etc. I was not under any contract with them and already felt like letting go, but without another income source, I had payments to make.

That day was different, I was invincible. $528 American was roughly $845 Canadian at the time. It was the most money I had made for two hours work in my life.

Rather than fire the clients, I just stopped answering the phone. It was kind of fun listening to the escalating anger in the voices of executives as they left me messages. It may not have been the best business move but I didn't care. I was burning bridges and loving it.

My day job was selling and delivering furniture for my dad. Because I worked in retail, my days off were during the week. That's why I started businesses on the side. None of my friends were taking Tuesday and Wednesday off.

I learned a lot in the years I worked for my dad. I wouldn't trade it for anything, but I also knew that I didn't want to be the owner of a furniture store.

I kept the day job for far too long because my blueprint was such that I thought I needed a 9 to 5 stable job. My adult entertainment business was making me the same amount in a month that my job paid in a year, before I finally quit. This all happened in the span of about six months.

While I kept my job, my girlfriend (now my wife) Claire, did the majority of the work. She built adult websites, spammed newsgroups, wrote copy and processed the incoming content licenses we purchased. Without her I'm not sure I would've had the same focus to scale.

Once I quit, we were able to focus 100% of our effort into our online business.

I noticed that the company we were processing our sales through was throwing an event in Las Vegas. I bought a ticket on the cheap and flew out last minute. My first business trip.

In hindsight I realize how important this trip was. When I got on the plane to leave Toronto I thought I was making enough money. When I got on the plane to come home I realized others were making far more money than me. It opened my eyes to the huge possibilities that could come from scaling.

Scaling meant purchasing thousands of porn images, building "feeder sites" to advertise our "money site" (more on that later) and linking them up to a large adult hub. There were more than enough images to be licensed but not enough hours in the day.

When I came home we worked very hard on building up our business. We were also approached by several people who wanted us to build porn sites for them. We threw out a ridiculously large number to see who would bite. Many did. We eventually used this money to put a down payment on our first home.

## Hiring Friends and Family

On vacation to the Cayman Islands Claire and I decided that in order for us to properly scale this, we needed to hire outside help. Neither of us had any real experience building a business so quickly, so we contracted friends and family members (not a wise move). This worked for us in the short-term. Keep in mind this was the late 1990s, many of our friends didn't even know how to use Windows 95. We had to send them on courses so they could learn to use computers and build porn sites for us.

Within a few months we had more than 10 people building websites for us from their homes. This quickly scaled our business, putting more money into our pockets than we were ever accustomed to. Before I knew it we had thousands of porn sites generating traffic for us.

We were taking expensive trips, throwing parties, gambling, shopping and enjoying life on a whole new level. I could get used to this.

I was always intrigued by how differently each of the people who built websites for us operated. Keep in mind these people were all given the same amount of training, and were paid a flat dollar amount for every website they built, with no upper limit on how much they could deliver.

Only one person had the foresight to hire additional help at a lower rate than we were paying to increase his billing and deliverables.

Most of them did the minimum amount they needed to sustain their current lifestyle. One couple loaded all their work into an extremely busy Sunday of building websites. That Sunday would cover the entire two weeks of their time.

It was definitely an interesting experiment, my expectation was that when everyone was given the ability to make an unlimited amount of money, they would all push hard. I have since learned that in order to get the most out of someone you need to set your expectations in advance and pay accordingly.

Unfortunately for us, this business model didn't last much longer than a year or two. Fortunately we made a lot of money in that timeframe. But of course as expected we had to cut loose the people who were building sites for us. We made sure they all had an opportunity to build their own businesses without help.

As it happens, when you close one chapter with your friends others tend to close as well. A big lesson for me was that I will never hire friends or family in the future. Not only has it not been good for me, I have seen it blow up for other entrepreneurs I'm friends with.

**My First Product**

In my online business, my major focus has always been traffic. Traffic is the term used to describe website visitors. The more traffic you get the more money you make. I rarely focused on creating a unique product of my own because it was easier to be an affiliate who gets paid a commission for sending customers to a third-party. I rarely had to deal with customer service, lawsuits, regulation or any other issues that the companies I sent traffic to were dealing with.

The first traffic method I employed is still used today in many circles. It's often referred to as feeder traffic or building feeder websites. People in the adult business were the first to use the strategy.

In 1999, I created my first product. It was called FreeXXXSpace and it allowed people with no web hosting options to place their websites with me in exchange for some top/bottom ad space. It was successful in the beginning but quickly became a burden.

The first problem was that without any contracts, I paid my hosting company to hire a programmer to code the project. Within no time I was outgrowing that hosting company. They didn't want to lose my business so they tried to hold the source code of my project for ransom.

Rather than giving in to their ransom, I started to move everything to my new hosting company in the background. I then purposely went 30 days behind on my $20,000 monthly hosting bill. In my opinion when someone tries to screw you, your only option is to screw back. I sent an employee to New Jersey to oversee the movement of our physical hardware. The hosting company was told once we had everything moved they would be handed a check.

Because they held their ground and tried to protect the source code we paid to have written, they never saw their last payment.

I was forced to shut down a profitable business because I didn't take the necessary steps to protect my source code.

I continued to work with my feeder site strategy while trying to come up with other ways to generate large volumes of traffic.

## P2P

Fast forward a few years, the P2P file-sharing revolution had already started thanks to Napster. Something I didn't expect, when Napster closed their doors, a half dozen competitors emerged. Further fueling the community of people who swapped media online. Software applications like LimeWire, Kazaa, and Bear Share were scooping up millions of downloads and building extremely large user bases.

In 2007 it was estimated that LimeWire was installed on one third of all PCs connected to the Internet. That meant access to tens if not hundreds of millions of people who would also be using LimeWire not only to download music and television shows, but also porn movies.

I began my obsession with P2P networks early. Not from the downloaders perspective. In fact I never downloaded any illegal content, mainly because it rarely matched the quality I was used to when purchasing. My obsession with the technology was based on the potential to generate traffic from such a large user group.

The challenges were huge.

1. I needed to find a way to get people from a downloaded video file over to a website.
2. I had to dominate my connections to these networks in order to maximize the downloads of those video files.
3. It needed to work financially since I was going to be taking on some hefty bandwidth charges.

My first experiments involved watermarking videos with website addresses in the hopes that people would type their way in and visit. Not likely.

Another friend of mine in the business was doing this with me in tandem. He quickly gave up while I continued to push forward. I wasn't sure myself if it was the right move but something told me to stay on it.

I started playing around with QuickTime, a video codec developed by Apple. The scripting language behind QuickTime allowed for clickable banners, dynamic advertising and even forced pop-up ads in the browser. I ran a small test, uploaded a few hundred movies to a DSL connection in my office running LimeWire, and waited.

Within 48 hours I generated a sale. The commission was $45. My cost to run a computer and Internet connection for the month was around $90. I figured I could make this work on a larger scale with a bit more work.

Within a few months, I was running a few dozen servers on high-capacity connections. The business was scaling nicely, but I needed help.

I partnered with a friend who was in the same business because he had access to a sales team that could help sell traffic. With his help, and the help of his staff we scaled the business very quickly.

After a while, I got bored and decided to sell my share of the company. They hired me back to consult with them for several months. Shortly after, some changes were made to the LimeWire network that made that business much harder to run. Although I felt bad for my colleagues who remained, I was happy that I made the exit when I did.

## S.E.O.

The next focus was going to be search engine optimization. I had partnered with someone who I was mentoring regarding traffic. I gave him an old domain and let him run with a search engine strategy while I paid the bills. I figured the worst case scenario would be that he would fizzle out. Within 10 months he had ranked in the top 10 for the word porn on Google.

This ushered in an ever-increasing flow of traffic and dollars into my business.

The strategy used was simple. It's referred to as ABC trading. Essentially to pull this off you need one website that you want to rank at the top and as many as 50 or 100 feeder sites that you use to trade traffic. Every site you trade traffic with gets a link from one of your feeder sites, and in exchange links to the one website that you want to rank. This website will not link back to anyone. It still works today, try it yourself :-)

Of course when you are racing to the top of Google, you might try to take some shortcuts. I know we did. We also paid for it.

After more than a year in the top 10 even reaching number one and often sitting in the number two position we were penalized for buying and selling links on our website. We went from 150,000 - 250,000 visitors daily to 10,000 - 15,000 visitors daily. It may still sound awesome to you, but our advertisers were not impressed.

This was a hard lesson, don't rely on a single point of free traffic to run your business. Google is not a traffic strategy unless you are buying advertising from them. Everything else is at the mercy of a simple algorithm change or broken rule. It can take a ton of effort to chase the dream of being number one for your term. And it can take a split second of poor judgment to yank the carpet out from below.

This change triggered the need for me to lay off staff, make extreme cutbacks within my business and personally rethink my future. For the first time in my career as an entrepreneur I didn't know what to do next.

**Herding Cats**

The adult business was becoming extremely difficult because everything was free. Unless you wanted to be in the business of working with models, it was very difficult to monetize any traffic.

I had an office space, so I decided why not try hiring a model?

Let's call her Brandy.

Let me start by saying I don't like hiring models, dealing with them, or being on that side of the business at all. But these were difficult times for my business and I was willing to lower my standards to keep things status quo.

Brandy started doing topless photos. Primarily the self shot style you see today. She wanted to keep things tasteful. They always do.

Within a month she was doing live cam shows complete with dildos, masturbation scenes, the works.

One day after moving from tasteful to slutty Brandy sent me an instant message in the middle of a live webcam show where she was naked and masturbating for an audience. The message exchange went something like this.

Brandy: "Um this is starting to feel like porn"
Me: "What did you think it was before now?"
Brandy: "I dunno I guess it just needed to be said"

And the shows continued.

The money was great, but the headaches were greater.

Stupidity. There's no nice way to say it, she was dumber than dirt and extremely manipulative. Constantly lying to us about things we didn't even care about. People think it's awesome to be in the adult business and deal with models. Nothing could be further from reality.

One day she called me in tears. Her boyfriend had beat her up. It was pretty bad.

When I went to pick her up, the evidence was all over her face. Someone had done a number on her.

I had two things to consider, her safety and my business. I decided to rent her an apartment so she could move out from her boyfriend. It also allowed for more WebCam time.

Within a few months, she got complacent with her free apartment and growing commission checks. She started to make demands, cancel shows etc. Then on my birthday she gave me an ultimatum. So I took the out. Paid her landlord and moved on.

Lucky for me her contract stated after a specified length of time not worked, the content and revenue would become the property of my company. I have since made a killing with her content.

## Going Mainstream

My adult business was dying faster than ever. My wife and I decided it was time to try something new, so we moved into mainstream. That's what the people in the adult business call what everyone else does :-)

We had so many failed attempts at bat. I thought it was going to be easier than adult. I was so wrong. My business was bleeding cash and I needed to plug the holes quickly.

I even tried a multilevel marketing product. I was able to generate thousands of leads and I still couldn't make it work.

I still knew how to generate traffic I was just spinning my wheels in the wrong direction.

One good thing that came from my association with the MLM product was a friendship and partnership with someone locally who just happened to be selling the same product. Neither of us is involved in that business anymore but we still do projects together today. I would gladly repeat that mistake again.

I eventually was able to start generating some affiliate revenue in the mainstream space, but it was still a difficult ride.

One thing I could still capitalize on was my search engine optimization knowledge. People were willing to pay thousands of dollars to hear me talk about how we got to the top for porn. I started running classes in my office. The information was solid and the people who put it into practice made good returns.

I knew there had to be a better way to scale my time. I had lots of methods for generating traffic, but I didn't want to be a full-time teacher.

In 2009 I discovered a website called the Warrior Forum. It was there, that I found a high demand for my knowledge. I could package it and sell it. This was scalable. Hundreds of thousands of people were visiting this website every month and they were all hungry for Internet marketing info products.

Within a short amount of time I was able to generate a fantastic amount of business by advertising there.

Today, I have over 300 products for sale on the Internet. Most of them don't require any effort on my part now that they are finished. Each one generates revenue for me on a regular basis.

I'd like to show you how I run a business that provides myself and my wife a comfortable lifestyle. A lifestyle that for me includes smoking pot daily.

# Chapter 2: Why I Smoke

I promise not to make this another pothead ramble about why marijuana should be legal.

I have smoked marijuana for my entire adult life. There's lots of competing information out there about whether or not it's good or bad for you. To be honest I don't really care. When I eat a cupcake, I don't worry about the calories. Instead I enjoy the fuck out of that cupcake. So when I smoke a joint, I don't worry about how it might affect my health. What it does for me in the moment is more important.

I don't drink. I'm not an alcoholic, I just don't like getting drunk. Sometimes I enjoy a glass of wine, or the occasional cocktail. But I would prefer to be high instead of drunk. I'm in much better control of my motor skills and what comes out of my mouth.

I also like to get high when I'm working. For many people it seems counterproductive. Especially if you don't do it often. I always picture the guy in the anti-drug commercials sitting on his sofa in his mom's basement unable to care about anything. I'm not that guy. I truly believe that most drugs and alcohol just amplify the person inside. If you can live in your mom's basement, smoking pot isn't going to change that. If you have higher expectations of your life, you can still smoke pot. I've proven that and so have many of my high functioning friends who also like to smoke pot.

People ask me how I come up with so many good ideas. I often reply by telling them I smoke pot. Most of the time they laugh and think I'm joking. Again, I'm not saying that smoking pot makes me creative. I was creative long before I discovered getting high, but getting high amplifies my creativity. Ask anyone who works with me. I can smoke a joint and then troubleshoot just about any problem and come up with a solution faster than anyone. Some people use caffeine, sugar, antidepressants, alcohol, vitamin B12 shots, steroids whatever to enhance their performance. My business requires me to use my brain in unconventional ways.

50 years ago, drinking and smoking in the office were completely acceptable. In fact drinking by executives was encouraged in many ad agencies, and other places where creativity was important. Of course getting drunk doesn't help you to solve problems or become more creative so it didn't do much except send executives home drunk so they could beat their wives.

I expect some people purchased this book based on the title. Some of you are already pot smokers and some of you probably thought to yourself: "if this pothead can run a successful online business, I can do it blindfolded".

Although I would never encourage illegal activity, if you are able to obtain it, I highly recommend you test this as a performance enhancer during times where you need to be creative. I am told in some places where marijuana is medically legal "writers cramp" is an acceptable affliction to suffer from in order to get a prescription.

# Chapter 3: It's Never Been Easier To Own A Business

The Internet has brought the world together in a way nobody had considered before.

If I wanted to write this book 20 years ago, I would've had a hell of a time publishing.

Self-publishing didn't exist, and I know mainstream publishing houses wouldn't touch this book. Even if I could get the book printed, I'd have to buy a minimum of 10,000 copies. And then of course I would have to find retailers to stock the book on consignment.

Today, I'm still making choices about how to publish, market and distribute this book. But all my choices are awesome because there are so many new distribution platforms available to me. I can also build a list of people just like you who are interested in running a business online and enjoying a little weed :-)

There's really no excuse today. It doesn't matter how narrow your audience, you can find them online.

Long before I published this book, I bought traffic from Facebook to build my list. I targeted people living in the United States, Canada, Australia and the United Kingdom. Oh yeah, those people also had to be potheads :-)

Guess how many self-confessed potheads there are in my target group? Over 5 million people. The funny part is for some reason, people in the United Kingdom clicked on my ads 3 times more often than anywhere else. What does that say about my UK based readers?

There has never been a time in history where I could market a newsletter and eventually a printed book to 5 million self-confessed potheads except for now.

My wife managed to target several million vegans on Facebook.

Every day new opportunities present themselves on the Internet. Those of us who spend our time working online recognize and exploit those opportunities whenever possible. You don't have to be a genius to pull this off. You just have to have an idea that's unique and cool. If other people like it they'll share it with their friends that also think it's cool.

The worst thing you could be doing with your life, is watching TV. It's designed to keep you entertained between working hours. Don't fall into the trap.

Some people have actually said to me "it's too late for me, the Internet's been around for a long time now making it hard for me to innovate"

Are you fucking serious?

The Internet as we know it is roughly 20 years old. Some geeks will argue with me. Stop being a geek Poindexter and let me make my point. When television was 20 years old, it was still black and white with very few channels and very crappy programming. TV stations didn't even run programs all day long. Most television sets still had a round screen with a giant wood box surrounding it.

Don't talk yourself out of anything or let anyone else talk you out of anything that you want to try. There is no such thing as market saturation unless you are selling refrigerators in the town that doesn't build new homes.

Think about how much television has changed since it was 20 years old. That's how new the Internet is. We are all still poking around in the dark testing things to see what works and what doesn't. There will always be room for new players who want to change the game. It doesn't mean you have to be a computer scientist or an engineer. You can be a pothead dropout like me, and never have to answer to a boss again.

Start carving out your audience today. We are waiting to be lead/entertained/educated and sold :)

# WHO'S IN YOUR CORNER?

# Chapter 4: Who's In Your Corner?

I wouldn't be where I am today without the support of my wife Claire. Not only does she put up with my shit, she supports me on just about every stupid idea I come up with. I believe it's our job to support each other in all of our dreams.

Often, when people are building a business they are doing it part-time. This usually means taking time away from your family. If your family doesn't believe in your dream, not only will they make it very difficult for you to succeed, it's also likely you will resent them when you do become successful. You can't have the person you've chosen to spend the rest of your life with doubting you.

When my wife Claire decided she wanted to write a cookbook I dove in and helped everywhere I could. I took photographs, designed the book cover, helped her with publishing and marketing, motivated her when she needed it and more. I expect her to help me just as much when I do things. Not only that, I am her biggest fan. I usually brag about her more than she does. That's why we have a good relationship, because we are rooting for each other.

If your relationship is similar to mine you can skip this chapter. Otherwise keep reading.

If you are in a situation where your significant other makes jokes about your business aspirations, refers to what you do as "playing on the computer", constantly interrupts you with nonessential things or just shows a lack of respect for what you are doing, it's time to have a talk.

The first talk you have to have is with yourself. Why are you building a business? Are you building a business, or are you tinkering?

It can be very difficult to admit, but I have worked with many people who have full-time jobs that fulfill them but are trying to build a business on the side. Some of these people use the side business as a distraction from their life. I'm clearly not a therapist, but if your business is a distraction you have bigger things to deal with than this book will cover. My advice is to seek help from a professional.

So let's assume that your true motivation for building your business is to create a better life for you and your family. My friend Justin Popovic became an entrepreneur shortly after his son was born. He genuinely wanted to set a better example for his son than working for a big company and being unhappy. His motivation was truly genuine. How could his wife possibly not support that? And of course she did which is why he is successful today.

So let's say you have a strong motivation for wanting to do this, and your significant other is still disrespecting you. You need to have a discussion with them explaining your motivation for building a business. You also need to explain how their comments make you feel. In many cases when dealing with family members who are disempowering with their questions or comments you can just keep them at a distance. Your partner or spouse is a different story. Explain to them that they need to be in your corner and rooting for you.

A simple analogy comes from sports. If you are on a baseball team and your spouse makes fun of your ability to play and then loudly makes jokes while you play, it's more likely you're going to lose than if your spouse cheering for you.

Of course it's a two-way street. You need to treat your spouse exactly the same way if you expect them to support you. If you haven't, you need to address it, apologize for it and ask for support going forward and promise the same. It seems so simple when you break it down but if you don't have this conversation there will be too much friction making success very difficult for you. More importantly, if you do manage to fight through and become successful your level of resentment for your spouse will be at an all-time high. We always look down on the people who doubted us when we make it. How dare they doubt us?

Some people like to frame this as good negative motivation. "I'll show them"

Although negative motivation can often be very powerful. The people closest to you need to be positively motivating you as well. Even if your cheering section is one person, you have a much better chance of being successful than if everyone thinks you will fail. We need someone who will celebrate with us in order to make success feel sweet.

# DON'T LET FEAR DICTATE

# Chapter 5: Don't Let Fear Dictate

Is fear your bitch? Or are you fear's bitch?

Are you afraid of failure?
How about success?

Maybe you're afraid that PayPal may close your account just at the moment you become successful. Maybe you're afraid of what your friends and family will say if you fail.

Have I scared you yet?

It's tough to be an entrepreneur, we have to take calculated risks every day. There is no place for fear but we all know it exists. So we can't just sweep it under the rug.

It's important to make sure that you recognize fear for what it is, and try not to let it guide your decision making process. Any entrepreneur who runs their business on fear will eventually die on the vine. It's often the things that scare us the most that pay the biggest dividends.

My mother-in-law is a classic example of someone who is driven by fear. I remember a few years ago my wife was building a successful video encoding company. She had more clients than she could handle and her business required a hefty capital equipment expense. Essentially she needed to buy 16 Mac Pro computers. After doing some research, we decided to lease the equipment over 3 years.

Casually over a family dinner, the topic came up. Rather than wishing her daughter all the best with her successful business, my mother-in-law immediately started asking what Anthony Robbins refers to as disempowering questions.

Are you sure you need that many computers?
What happens if your business dries up before the lease runs out?

The above questions are based on fear. If you start asking yourself what happens when you go out of business or when money stops coming in, you know fear is driving the conversation. You don't need to go there, when you do you can deal with the problem. Until then figure out how to keep as much money as you can while making sure you fund growth.

A friend of mine started a clothing line a few years ago. One day we were going out for lunch and I asked him how things were going.

Steve: "Well I have all my suppliers sorted out, all my designs done and all my samples in hand. All I have to do now is find retailers and distributors for my product. In fact the biggest trade show in my industry hits Las Vegas in 4 months."

Me: "Have you secured your booth space yet?"

Steve: "Well no… Frankly it's too expensive. By the time I pay for my booth and my travel it will be close to $4000. I suppose I could put it on my credit card and hope for the best but that would be stupid."

Me: "If I were you I would do exactly that."

What seems more stupid?

Starting a company, creating a product and then sitting on your hands?
Or
Taking advantage of a low interest credit card to put your product in front of buyers?

I believe my friend was making his decision based on fear. Not just fear of his credit card bill, although that is a very real fear which I'll talk about in a minute, but I believe his fear was more about the fact that if he made that decision he would be forced into a sink or swim position.

Often people like to pretend they are in business. They're in startup mode for years. They love to talk to their friends about their products, post pictures on Facebook but never really make any waves. I think the scariest thing for these people is discovering whether or not they have a real business. If you aren't willing to put your product in front of buyers, you are probably scared to learn the truth about how well it will sell. Maybe deep down you don't think it is awesome as your friends and family do. Otherwise what are you so scared of?

So let's talk about financial fear because it's easily the most scary of them all. At least for those of us that live in the first world. I mean there are millions of people who are afraid they may not eat dinner tonight or have access to clean water tomorrow morning. But they won't be reading this book.

A lot of people who are getting started in business will try to go to their bank with a business plan and ask for a bank loan. Very rarely do they get one. And often when they do it comes with tons of stipulations including personal guarantees, like the bank manager approving expenses over $1000 or sometimes they will require you to take out a life insurance policy through their preferred insurer etc.

The reason why they try and get a business loan is because they think they are protected if the business goes bankrupt. For the most part the bank will force you to personally guarantee the money either way. So now you have a bank loan that you personally guarantee and you have to ask your bank manager for permission to write checks. You just got fucked.

You would be much better suited to go and take out a line of credit on your home or use low interest credit cards to cover your business expenses early on. You're still borrowing the money except the interest rate is lower and you don't have to deal with a dummy bank manager on every business decision. And trust me these guys are stupid. That's why they are bank managers and not entrepreneurs.

Of course when it comes to borrowing any money people get scared. They are afraid they might end up in deep debt or even worse bankruptcy. Mainly it's because we live in a society with values that are fucked up. We actually believe it to be shameful when someone can't pay their debts. To the point where we are afraid to go into debt ourselves for the internal shame we will feel.

I have felt the shame myself and I know it to be very real. The good news is, you don't need to be ashamed if things don't work out. Because most countries have privacy laws protecting you from shame. In North America, it's very easy to renegotiate debt with your creditors.

I've been in situations where things got a little heavy on the credit side. Without going into too much detail let me just say this. If you go more than 90 days without paying your credit card bills, your credit card company is usually willing to settle for $0.40 on the dollar. They will also freeze your interest and allow you to pay back in installments. Of course this means you won't be able to get credit for a while but that's not the worst thing in the world either.

Not being able to get credit in this day and age does not lock you out of anything. We have prepaid credit cards, lots of ways to get car loans without credit etc. you won't suffer, certainly not as much as someone who can't get clean water ;-)

The last thing I'll leave you with regarding credit fear is this. People often keep credit available for several things. Often they'll use it for things they want like a vacation or new wardrobe. The ultraconservative people will keep their credit cards for emergencies only. Expensive repair bills etc.

If you are trying to start a business, you are trying to make a better life for yourself and your family. I can think of no bigger emergency than trying to build a better life. Because you only get one. And when you die nobody cares how much money you owe the bank.

# THE VALUE OF YOUR IDEAS

# Chapter 6: The Value Of Your Ideas

Hopefully you are full of good ideas. That will make being an entrepreneur very easy.

It will be even easier when you understand that those ideas have little to no value at all while they are still just ideas.

I remember once a business colleague and I were having lunch. He told me he had a great new idea for a piece of software. When I asked him what the software was going to do, he told me that I would need to sign a nondisclosure/non-compete agreement if I wanted to hear more.

I politely told him I did not want to hear more about his idea. He proceeded to tell me anyway. The idea was great, but someone still needed to write the software, come up with the name, test it, market it, support it and update it. Chances are very slim someone is going to steal your idea when none of the work has been done to prove it even works.

If you want someone to invest in your idea or partner with you or possibly expose your product to their customers you need to be willing to prove your concept or nobody will take you seriously. Don't talk about your ideas. Not only do they not have value, people who talk in ideas are usually not action takers. When people come to me with an idea I tell them to go away and come back with the concept done.

Everybody has ideas. The value comes in how you execute them. There are a lot of killer projects being worked on right now. No matter how amazing and cool you may think your idea is, it's probably already been done by someone else. So in order to make people notice, you need to actually make your idea work.

I'll give you a different example.

Many years ago I was an affiliate for a large adult processor. They asked their top affiliates to attend a summit at the Four Seasons hotel in Chicago. They flew me out, put me up in a nice room and paid for all my expenses, meals etc.

I was there with a group of 8 other affiliates from around the world. The purpose of the trip was simple, they wanted our ideas. We were their biggest affiliates making the most money for them. And they were one of our top sources of revenue. It only made sense for us to help each other.

I gave them an idea that made them over $20 million in 6 months. The idea itself was something I was doing in my own business. But it wasn't a $20 million idea to me because I didn't have the customer base that they did.

My idea was only valuable to them and their resources, and its value wasn't realized until they implemented the idea which costed them time and money to prove.

Don't be afraid to share ideas that may be more valuable to others than you. It helps to raise your profile. So when you talk people listen. That's more valuable than being the guy who won't speak without a contract.

# CREATING INTANGIBLES

# Chapter 7: Creating Intangibles

My entire business online is dedicated to creating and selling intangible products. There are a few things that make the tangible list as well but I'll get into that later.

An intangible product is something that is created once and distributed an unlimited amount of times electronically. This could be software, music, photography, artwork or a simple downloadable e-book or guide.

Intangible products have become extremely popular recently with the advent of portable devices like iPad, Kindle etc. it's never been easier to distribute your content electronically. People have proven they are willing to pay for electronic content, and in many cases they are willing to pay more for electronic content than they do for physical content.

At the top of my list, software is one of my most favorite products to create. I'm not a programmer, but I understand programming enough to be able to work with programmers and design software specification documents that they can use. So the idea comes from me but the actual work is done by a professional software developer.

We live in a world where people spend the majority of their day on a computer. If you can find a way to save someone a few minutes, or compress a few steps into one, you will make money selling software. I don't care if you have a new search engine optimization tool or if you figured out a way to make a better grocery list. There is an audience who wants to buy your software.

Software is awesome because the people who buy it become your customer base and they start to share their ideas with you for making your software even better. Listen to their ideas, survey them to find out what their needs are. Then every 6 to 12 months you can release an upgraded version of your software and charge accordingly. A good percentage of your user base will pay for that upgrade.

If you have an idea for a good piece of software you will need a few things in order to have that software created.

The first thing you need is called a wireframe. These are extremely easy to create. You can do it using a spreadsheet application, pencil and paper, or a wire framing tool which you can easily find with a Google search.

A wireframe is essentially a skeleton of your application. What does each screen look like? What does the user see the first time they open your software? What do they see when they want to change options? What screen are they taken to when they click each button?

Most of my wireframes will show a minimum 10 to 20 screens based on different variables and inputs the user might deal with.

The next thing you need is a specification document. This document outlines what the software is going to do and how it should be done. I will refer to various screen diagrams from the wireframe throughout the specification document. All of this may sound complicated but it's actually extremely easy.

The more detail you provide your programmer the less headaches you will have later. I highly recommend putting together a very complete wireframe and specification document. And then hand those documents over to a few friends who have strong technical backgrounds and ask for their opinion. Sometimes ideas will pop up before you give it to your programmer.

The last thing you'll need to know is the environment you want your software to run. Would this be a mobile application? Exclusive to the iPad? Desktop software? Or server software?

If your software is designed to run on your server, in other words people will reach it through their web browser, it requires a whole lot less testing than if it will run on the desktop. Desktop software can be very lucrative but it can also be very buggy. If you don't have a dedicated computer for each operating system and every version of the operating system to test, you will have to release your software in beta at first to get testing results.

If it's designed to run on a specific device, you will need that device to test your software. Chances are if it works on your device it will work on all devices like yours. So again testing is kept to a minimum.

I could go on forever about why software is awesome but I will leave you with this. Not very many people develop software because of the detail, testing etc. Most people see it as too difficult. I like to operate in places where competition is at a minimum and the payoffs are high. This is one of those places.

If you are a musician, taking your career online has never been easier. There are so many ways that you can market yourself online.

I have a coaching client who is a very good musician, he takes his music seriously and plays several nights a week to live audiences. He doesn't have a day job, and he has built a recording studio in his home that rivals many expensive studios.

On our very first call I asked him if he ever considered recording loop packages for people who use software like Apple's GarageBand. Surprisingly he had never considered this option. The good news is there are millions of people using music software like this. Many of them are looking for additional sets of music loops to stack and make their own music.

For those of you who don't know, a loop is essentially a few seconds of music that can be played over and over again in the loop like a drumbeat or a repeated guitar riff. When stacked together, amateur composers can make unique music by choosing different sets of loops to play together. The demand for loops grows every day.

Maybe you don't see yourself as a mercenary for hire. Instead you would rather see your band become extremely popular. Have you ever heard of a rapper named 50 Cent?

50 had a record deal. He was about to make it big until he got shot several times in the chest. His record company didn't think he would recover and dropped his contract like a hot potato. 50 struck back by giving away all of his music for free on the Internet. He created so much demand for himself that record companies fought over him.

Giving away your music for free when you are struggling is one of the best strategies you can use to find your audience. The traditional way most musicians do this is to their websites and MySpace pages. I recommend a slightly different distribution strategy.

I like to take advantage of peer to peer file sharing applications like BitTorrent. Start by making a list of the musicians who influence you and your style. Chances are fans of those artists will also like your work.

Using standard MP3 software you can tag your songs with artists names after your own. The average rap song will have 3 or 4 contributed artists named in the artist field. By adding the artists names who influence your music after your own, you're able to capitalize on the people who are searching for music by those artists. If you're distributing hip-hop music that sounds similar to Dr. Dre. Put your band name first and then say influenced by: Dr. Dre in the artist field. Immediately you're going to pick up millions of people searching for Dr. Dre's music.

If you write content like how-to guides, e-books etc. this is still a very lucrative business. Especially if you could fill a need in a market that is desperate. Some of the best selling e-books I have seen offer home remedies for things like yeast infections.

Whenever you can find a group of desperate buyers who need your solution, you will make money.

One of the things I like about selling downloadable books today is that it's actually really easy to bridge the gap from intangible to tangible. Amazon.com owns a company called Create Space. This company allows you to upload your electronic book in PDF format, and then publish a physical book on Amazon using their own print on demand service. Amazon handles the printing of your book, payment processing, shipping and customer service. Paying you a direct royalty on every unit sold.

In fact a deal like this will net you much more money per unit than you could ever make working with a traditional publishing company.

Having a physical version of your book available lends credibility to the electronic version. Most people don't realize that you can create a print on demand book so easily these days. So they still put a lot of value on a product that is available physically through Amazon. I have seen many people sell more e-books by putting a little Amazon link under their payment link for downloads to increase the perceived value.

The other cool thing about having your book on Amazon is that you can leverage their own traffic and affiliate system. Having a book with a title matching popular search terms will make ranking very easy. Google likes ranking Amazon pages. So promoting your Amazon pages leads to faster search engine optimization results. Plus it's just another sales channel for you.

When it comes to selling your e-book there are a few choices. Amazon also has a Kindle publishing platform that allows you to publish to the Kindle e-reader. Again this is a no-brainer.

Additionally you will want to have a website dedicated to selling your e-book. This website should contain all the information about why someone would want to buy your book along with links to make a payment and get an instant download.

You will want to use a website like 99designs.com to have your book cover created and website designed. Sites like this offer a crowd sourcing solution that allows multiple designers to create concepts for you without getting paid. You choose from dozens of design concepts. The designer whose concept you choose gets the money. It's one of the coolest ways to get exactly what you want designed on the cheap.

In order to process payments for your e-book you will want to work with a payment platform that allows affiliates to promote your product. Affiliates are like salespeople. I often pay a 55% bounty on every sale to my affiliates. They're doing all my sales and marketing work for me, so I'm quite happy to give up a large percentage of each sale as a reward.

If you write a book about how to get 6 pack abs, and it's selling well on its own, chances are other people who sell fitness and diet books and have customer lists will be interested in e-mailing those customers about your product. Offering your product through affiliate networks like clickbank.com makes things easy. You don't have to do any accounting or send out any checks. Click Bank does it for you. Sending you your royalties and paying your affiliates on your behalf.

I highly recommend you create a product based on something you are already interested in or are intimately familiar with. Don't write a book about yeast infections just because I said it was a good niche. If you've never had a yeast infection and you're not a doctor you shouldn't be writing books about yeast infections.

If you are however really good at picking up girls then of course you should be looking in that direction because it's likely you actually have some techniques of your own that haven't been exposed by other pickup artists who wrote books of their own. If you have a really good technique for putting up drywall, chances are people will buy that. Especially if it solves a problem for newbie do-it-yourselfers.

I can tell you from my own experience that whenever you try and jump into a category that doesn't interest you or isn't something you know backwards and forwards you will get bored long before it's a real business. Save yourself the headache, stick to what you know and what interests you. It will never feel like work.

# WHITE LABEL & PRIVATE LABEL

# Chapter 8: White Label and Private Label

So lets say you are too lazy, or not motivated to create your own product. That's cool. You still have lots of options.

Many companies offer products under private labeling contracts. The easiest way to explain this is to talk about supplements. There are companies today that will formulate supplements, sports drinks, protein powders, gels, bars, whatever with your name on it. There are websites today that allow you to mix and match list of ingredients to create your own formulated supplement. Then, upload your graphics and order a minimum of around 100 bottles and you have your own supplement company. Anytime you need more bottles, just order the wholesale amount you need and they are shipped to you. Some of these companies will even drop ship direct to your customers negating the need for you to have a warehouse.

In my world, I purchase private label rights to content I use online. I can buy entire e-books, videos, articles, software or audio files. Often created by experts, this content can be modified and I may claim to be the author. In fact, all of the Chronic Marketer White Papers were created using private label rights e-books I purchased from my friend Justin's business bestqualityPLR.com. His stuff is so good that we didn't need to change anything. The white papers were essentially lessons in basic Internet marketing. Stuff that a lot of new people can learn from but would bore me to tears if I had to write about.

Purchasing private label rights content is so simple. All you have to do is Google the type of content you are looking for with the initials PLR afterwards and start clicking.

I do recommend, if you're going to use private label rights content you ensure that the quality is what your customers should expect. Don't just blindly copy and paste text without reading it. There are many companies selling private label rights content written by authors whose second language is English. In many cases this content reads very poorly and won't pass muster.

Once you find content you want to work with, my suggestion is to edit it and style it your own way. Make sure to add footnotes or include your own tips as you are reading through to make it your own. In many cases there will be opportunities for you to embed affiliate links in your content. It's also a good idea to combine multiple private label rights products on the same subject.

I know people who make their living combining various private label rights products and editing them into a single book. They then publish that book on Amazon Kindle or as a paperback using print on demand publishing. There's a good market for this if you know how to come up with compelling book titles.

There are many cases where private label rights content will come in handy. But I don't recommend using it for your core products. I wrote every word of this book on my own. You wouldn't be very happy if you purchased this book and discovered the inside was written by someone else and the content was available everywhere.

Use it to educate and warm-up prospects who aren't quite ready for your products. That's the best use of digital private label rights products.

There are also affiliate programs that offer white label versions of their website. The best example would be a dating company. Rather than sending your visitors to a separate website, a dating company can white label a version of their website with your logo to match your style. Users feel like they are accessing something exclusive. And more importantly, you maintain your own brand image throughout the purchase experience. When a purchase is made, you get your commission as you would with any affiliate sale, and the dating site handles all the customer service. The only real difference being the customer never feels like they've left your website.

Using white label websites can be very effective for affiliates who already have a strong online presence.

# DON'T LET YOUR EGO DICTATE PRICING

# Chapter 9: Don't Let Your Ego Dictate Pricing

So you've created your intangible product. Maybe it's a piece of software, a course, videos, a book whatever.

Now you have to attach a price to your product. How much do you sell it for?

What a lot of people will do is compare their product to a competitor's product. Often assessing the thud factor. In other words "they have 5 videos and I have 7, I have audio recordings and transcripts they don't." That sort of thing.

Your price should be dictated by one thing and one thing only. Testing.

If at the end of the day, you can make more total dollars by selling your product for $1 than you can selling it for $47, why would you sell it for any price other than $1?

This is a rookie move, but I see people who make a lot of money making this mistake every day. All that matters is how much you make at the end of each day. I don't care how awesome you think your product is, how you want to position it, how much time you put into it or anything else. As my good friend Mark Lyford says, "business is a game and money keeps the score." Don't take any less than the maximum amount of money each day.

So the question always comes up: "what if one of my customers purchases at a higher price while I am testing different price variants?"

First of all if you are using the right split testing software, your customers will always see the same sales page they purchased from. On the odd chance they find it at a different price, you take care of your customer and make sure they are refunded the difference. No big deal. How many times have you purchased something only to find it cheaper a few days later? We have grown to accept this as consumers.

It doesn't matter because you are finding the best way to make the most money every day, a few customer service hiccups during this process is to be expected.

You're in the digital downloads business. It doesn't cost you anything to deliver your product. Don't let ego or pride dictate any of this. As long as your advertising dollars generate a profit, pick the pricing that makes you the most money. I don't care how awesome you think your product is, and neither does your customer.

How much does it cost to produce a hit song? Likely more than your product, and that song sells for $0.99

The only time this rule does not apply is when selling your time. Never undercut the value of your hours.

# WRITING SALES COPY

# Chapter 10: Writing Sales Copy

Probably one of the most overlooked yet most important things you can do on your website is crafting effective sales copy.

The text on a website is often an afterthought. Designers build websites using something called lorem ipsum text. It is essentially a bunch of fake paragraphs used to represent where text should be placed in the design. Often, the job of filling in this text is left to an inexperienced business owner.

You can write your own sales letter, or you can hire a professional copywriter to do it for you. But no matter what you do, text should always come before design. Make sure you know exactly what you want your website to communicate and how you want to sell that to your customer. It's not about your logo, color scheme, fonts, HTML 5 whatever. All that matters are the words you use to communicate with your prospect.

We've all seen these ugly websites with what seem to be 30 page sales letters. Everyone says they hate them. But the funny thing is, the marketers who use them know that they work. There is a saying in copywriting which goes like this "length implies strength". Chances are your prospect will not read your entire sales letter, but they will stop at headlines and testimonials that interest them.

The headline is the most important part of any sales letter. Again this component is often overlooked. I am not a professional copywriter but in my experience here is what I've seen work.

Talk to me and sell me on the result. I don't care about how many colors your product comes in right now. All I care about is what it will do for me. And if the first words I read don't solidify my high hopes, I'm gone.

When I say talk to me, I mean try to use the words "you" and "your" as much as possible. Never talk in general terms about how other people love your product in your headline. Tell me why I will love it. The more often I use the words you and your throughout my sales copy, the better it converts (to a sale). Obviously without going overboard. People like to be talked to and told what to expect. The more honest and direct you are with them the better.

Traditional sales copy usually follows the format of a letter to a friend, often telling a story involving a struggle of some kind and how that struggle was overcome. With the help of a product of course. Often, a list of product benefits and features follows, then some frequently asked questions, a handful of good testimonials, a guarantee, an order box, some bonuses, another order box and a signature from the product creator and usually a photo.

For a long time, I resisted this format. Coming from the adult business I thought things could be done with a little bit more flair. I also thought that I could force people into a more modular style website where they could choose the information they wanted to read. I was so wrong. That is until I realized how to maintain a bit of difference.

Recently I broke the mold when it came to sales copy. One day after smoking a few joints, I came up with the idea to create sales copy that was graphically enhanced to look more like a newspaper or info graphic. I would place headlines and images in boxes, along with additional information sort of like the classified section of a newspaper or maybe an ad for an electronic shop. This sales copy was designed for a new business I was starting with my partner Justin Popovic. Neither of us was sure it was going to work and we were prepared to scrap it if nobody was biting.

What ended up happening, not only sparked a new business for Justin and I selling drip fed affiliate blogs, it also gained me a little notoriety among my peers. Before I knew it everything I was creating was in this style. So far I have created roughly a dozen sales letters using this new style. I'm going to include some graphics at the end of this chapter to illustrate.

I do believe you can bring your own style to sales copy, and by doing so you can be unique and stand out. People like pattern interrupts. When they go to a sales letter that follows a traditional format that they've seen too often they can be thrown off. By creating your own style but still following simple sales copy principles, you can do extremely well.

Just remember that sales copy is about persuasion, not manipulation. You are doing everything you can to convince your prospect that your product is worth purchasing. That can be solidified in a negative and a positive way and it's often a good idea to do both. Knowing who your product is for is important because you can list it off on your sales copy. It often works just as well to list who the product may not be for. The more your prospect sees that they fit into the box of your perfect customer, the more comfortable they will be making a purchase.

On the next few pages are some examples of document and sales copy design I have developed for my own projects. You will see sales copy for Drip Blogs, Content Primer, Vegan Flush and some of the Chronic Marketer White Papers.

I design everything using vector clip art, vector drawings from my cartoonist and any other needed graphics. Vector means computer drawings that are infinitely scaleable and print beautifully.

I design all my documents in Keynote for the Mac. It's actually designed for slide presentations but I find it's ability to handle fonts, vectors and export high resolution PDF's to be unmatched. Not to mention the entire iWork suite for the Mac is something like $99.

You might be asking now that you've read this, "how do the search engines recognize all your graphical text?"

The reality is, I don't write or design my website for search engines and neither should you. I don't care how Google sees my websites or sales copy because I buy traffic and leverage affiliates to help me sell my products. One of the biggest mistakes people make is writing sales copy to make it search engine friendly. Every time I see this done, the sales copy is terrible and won't convert or convince anyone.

Speak to your audience, entertain them and make them want to continue reading. It's your best shot at selling them.

GRAB YOUR 100% UNIQUE RECIPE BLOGS - YOU CHOOSE FROM 50 DIFFERENT CATEGORIES
DRIP FED RECIPE BLOGS
CHECK OUT ALL OF THESE LOW COMPETITION KEYWORDS
| SEARCH PHRASE | MONTHLY SEARCHES | SEARCH PHRASE | MONTHLY SEARCHES |
| --- | --- | --- | --- |
| beer recipe | 246,000 | orange recipe | 246,000 |
| banana recipe | 823,000 | peach recipe | 201,000 |
| carrot recipe | 368,000 | potato recipe | 1,500,000 |
| corn recipe | 673,000 | salmon recipe | 673,000 |
| coconut recipe | 368,000 | shrimp recipe | 673,000 |
| ham recipe | 368,000 | tuna recipe | 368,000 |
50 CATEGORIES WITH UP TO
2681 AUTOMATED BLOG POSTS
CHOOSE YOUR MICRO NICHE AND DOMINATE IT
The above chart shows 12 random selections from our 50 recipe categories. Each recipe category presents an excellent niche marketing opportunity. Here is your chance to build a blog that runs on total autopilot, updates daily and caters to a massive search audience with low competition.
While some markets go up and down with the times and the economy, other markets remain unchanged. This is one of them. People NEED to eat and the majority of people prepare their own food at home. Get bookmarked as one of your reader's go-to sites by providing them with tons of great recipes on an ongoing basis.
SHINY IS OUT
FAD PROOF & TREND PROOF
CHECK OUR SAMPLE RECIPE BLOG MAKINGSANDWICHES.COM
This is exactly how your blog will look delivered. Complete with ads for top ClickBank offers from Brad Gosse and New York Times best selling cookbook author Ron Douglas
WHAT YOU GET
100% UNIQUE RECIPE DRIP BLOG
These blogs are pre-loaded with Hundreds or thousands of blog posts. A new recipe every day. This makes it easy to build a mailing list using free services like feedburner.com
A BLOG THAT RUNS ON AUTOPILOT
All blog posts are pre-set to run and publish automatically. This means you have absolutely no work to do and you can still reap the rewards of a fresh, constantly updating, constantly growing blog in your highly targeted recipe niche.
BUILT IN AFFILIATE LINKS MAKE MONEY
You don't have to worry about getting your affiliate links, uploading banners, writing swipe copy or anything else that requires time and effort. Just give us your Clickbank ID and your custom blog will be automatically built to promote proven Clickbank products.
These blogs are 100% YOUR asset. Make money with additional banner ads, selling ad space, sponsored blog posts, paid ads to your RSS subscribers, flip the site on Flippa or even setting up a local recipe/cooking sites in your town and sell custom advertising packages to local restaurants.
CHOOSE FROM CATEGORIES WITH UP TO 7 YEARS OF UPDATES
THE NUMBER OF RECIPES = THE NUMBER OF DAYS YOUR BLOG WILL UPDATE
★AVOCADO 486
★GROUND BEEF 2981
★BEEF 915
★CHICKEN BREAST 2681
★BROCCOLI 427
★SPAGHETTI 919
★PASTA 798
★PIZZA 434
★RICE 973
★PORK 984
★TUNA 337
★SALMON 373
★CRAB 445
★POTATO 1981
★SWEET POTATO 400
★HAM 588
★BACON 436
★CAKE 2444
★BLACK BEAN 404
★YOGURT 792
★CARROT 368
★CHILI 432
★SHRIMP 574
★SAUSAGE 398
★SPINACH 330
★CUCUMBER 579
★CABBAGE 544
★STEW 487
★PUMPKIN 630
★SOUP 1718
★BANANA 546
★APPLE 1165
★ORANGE 682
★CHOCOLATE 1834
★PEACH 454
★SANDWICH 487
★COCONUT 414
★SALSA 890
★MUSHROOM 673
★SQUASH 425
★CRANBERRY 390
★MAYONNAISE 2181
★BEER 387
★WINE 2488
★ITALIAN 438
★EGG 748
★SOY 2078
★CORN 823
★LEMON 802
★GREEN BEANS 1239
★MORE BEING ADDED
These blogs are pre-loaded with recipe related blog posts from the recipe category of your choice. The content includes ingredients and directions with focused keywords for each category of recipe. You can cater to people with a huge variety of tastes
HOW DOES IT WORK?
1 Register a new domain or use one you already own and change the name servers to ours. (don't worry we will help)
2 Provide a few details like your ClickBank ID, desired title and description, recipe category keywords to link etc. (it couldn't be simpler)
3 Now that your blog is done, you can add links to your blogroll, edit advertising, add more blog posts, promote, link build or just kick back and...
RELAX
WE DO ALL THE WORK. YOU GET A FINISHED BLOG
WE'LL HOST IT FREE FOR LIFE. OR YOU CAN MOVE IT TO YOUR OWN HOST
FULLY CUSTOMIZABLE
NOOB FRIENDLY
As mentioned above, everything is literally done-for-you. Aside from the 3 steps above, you have no other work to do.
THOUSANDS OF KEYWORD COMBINATIONS MILLIONS OF POTENTIAL BUYERS
Recipe blogs attract a large number of women. This is your opportunity to build a list that can be sold everyday products like diet and fitness offers, cookbook offers, CPA offers, coupon sites etc.
ONE TIME FEE
No monthly or annual fees to pay. Ever.
THIS OFFER IS TIME SENSITIVE
The longer you wait the more you pay.
In the last month, one of our recipe blogs received
80,859 PAGE VIEWS
All of which was free traffic using methods we teach

DO I HAVE TO USE YOUR FREE HOSTING FOR LIFE PACKAGE?
Our service is setup to build your blog on our servers. Your hosting is free for life but if you want to move your hosting to your own server after we have set everything up, you are free to do so :)
NO DUPLICATE CONTENT HASSLES
First, each blog is setup with a randomly sequenced set of blog posts. The title of each blog post will also change randomly. In essence, every buyer of this service will have a 100% unique blog.
Second, the duplicate content concern will not be a legit concern. Just like news agencies syndicate the same news release from a wire service, your site will syndicate content (in a random order) from it's own database.
HOW MUCH MONEY CAN I MAKE WITH THIS?
Although we can't make guarantees for expected earnings, have a look at the Google analytics screenshot below representing one of our recipe blogs. If you earned an average of $10 CPM you might make $9,600 annually on this single blog.
Visitors Overview
Dec 29, 2011 - Jan 28, 2012
31,763 people visited this site
36,167 Visits
31,763 Unique Visitors
80,859 Pageviews
2.24 Pages/Visit
00:01:51 Avg. Time on Site
58.22% Bounce Rate
84.54% % New Visits
84.60% New Visitor
15.40% Returning Visitor
The above example blog has benefited from the promotional work outlined in our included free training
WHEN WILL MY BLOG BE READY?
After you purchase, you will be directed to a blog setup survey. Once you complete and submit the survey, your order is immediately received by us. Please allow 3-5 business days for your blog to be delivered as we are very busy helping customers with this offer.
Okay this offer seems too good to be true...
WHAT'S THE CATCH?
There is no catch! Although these blogs are 100% controlled by you, much of the pre-loaded content helps promote an affiliate program we own so we make money when you make sales. So, you still get access to a great affiliate marketing opportunity, we subsidize the cost of blog setup and hosting by partnering with you on our own offers. In other words... We win when you win :)
HOW THIS IS PERFECT FOR OFFLINE MARKETERS
Register your local town name along with a recipe keyword or cooking term. Sell full-page ads to local restaurants and cookware stores. Or sell the finished website to an off-line business for 10 times what you pay here.
HOW THIS IS PERFECT FOR AFFILIATE MARKETERS
Plug in your favorite Clickbank, CPA, CPL or adsense ads or just leave the high converting cookbook download offers in place. Easily outsource your traffic generation using our training.
MORE MONEY MAKING OPPORTUNITIES
These blogs are 100% YOUR asset. Make money with additional banner ads, selling ad space, sponsored blog posts, paid ads to your RSS subscribers, flip the site on Flippa and more. It's your blog to do with as you see fit.
SELL YOUR MATURE SITES FOR A PROFIT
SO ALL OF THIS SOUNDS GREAT, ESPECIALLY WHEN YOU CONSIDER THE VALUE
$99
Average (low end) cost to set up a blog of this nature.
$4,145
Cost to have 829 recipes written by low level writers on Fiverr.com (and they wouldn't be nearly as good)
$60
Average (low end) cost to host your blog for a single year.
TOTAL VALUE $4,304. BUT YOU WON'T PAY ANYWHERE NEAR THAT
IT'S A GREAT DEAL @ $997
ANYONE WOULD GLADLY PAY $497
YOU MIGHT WONDER IF WE'D GO AS LOW AS $297
HOW LOW CAN WE GO?
NOT EVEN $197
HAPPY NEW YEAR
LET'S MAKE 2012 THE BEST YEAR EVER
YOUR FRIENDS BRAD GOSSE AND JUSTIN POPOVIC
CLICK THE BUY BUTTON BELOW TO GET STARTED
BRAD AND JUSTIN WANT TO HELP YOU BRING IN THE NEW YEAR SUCCESSFULLY
THE FIRST 500 BUYERS WILL RECEIVE A MASSIVE DISCOUNT

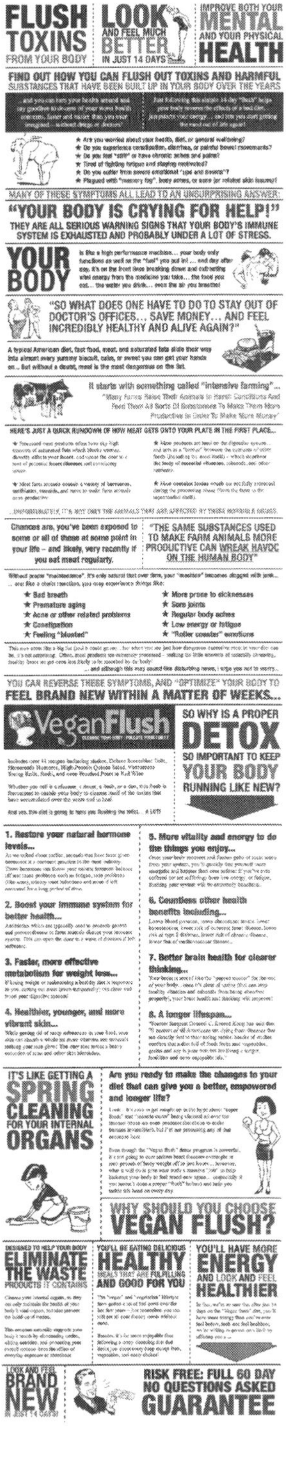
FLUSH TOXINS FROM YOUR BODY
LOOK AND FEEL MUCH BETTER IN JUST 14 DAYS
IMPROVE BOTH YOUR MENTAL AND YOUR PHYSICAL HEALTH
FIND OUT HOW YOU CAN FLUSH OUT TOXINS AND HARMFUL SUBSTANCES THAT HAVE BEEN BUILT UP IN YOUR BODY OVER THE YEARS
MANY OF THESE SYMPTOMS ALL LEAD TO AN UNSURPRISING ANSWER:
"YOUR BODY IS CRYING FOR HELP!"
THEY ARE ALL SERIOUS WARNING SIGNS THAT YOUR BODY'S IMMUNE SYSTEM IS EXHAUSTED AND PROBABLY UNDER A LOT OF STRESS.
YOUR BODY
"SO WHAT DOES ONE HAVE TO DO TO STAY OUT OF DOCTOR'S OFFICES... SAVE MONEY... AND FEEL INCREDIBLY HEALTHY AND ALIVE AGAIN?"
It starts with something called "intensive farming"...
"THE SAME SUBSTANCES USED TO MAKE FARM ANIMALS MORE PRODUCTIVE CAN WREAK HAVOC ON THE HUMAN BODY"
YOU CAN REVERSE THESE SYMPTOMS, AND "OPTIMIZE" YOUR BODY TO FEEL BRAND NEW WITHIN A MATTER OF WEEKS...
VeganFlush
SO WHY IS A PROPER DETOX SO IMPORTANT TO KEEP YOUR BODY RUNNING LIKE NEW?
IT'S LIKE GETTING A SPRING CLEANING FOR YOUR INTERNAL ORGANS
WHY SHOULD YOU CHOOSE VEGAN FLUSH?
ELIMINATE THE WASTE
HEALTHY
YOU'LL HAVE MORE ENERGY AND LOOK AND FEEL HEALTHIER
LOOK AND FEEL BRAND NEW IN JUST 14 DAYS!
RISK FREE: FULL 60 DAY NO QUESTIONS ASKED GUARANTEE

STOP LETTING REFUNDERS USE YOUR PRODUCTS AFTER PROCESSING
ELIMINATE ILLEGAL SHARING OF YOUR DOWNLOADS
SECURE YOUR CONTENT
FINALLY A SOLUTION FOR PRODUCT CREATORS THAT HELPS YOU
IT'S LIKE HIRING SOMEONE TO POLICE YOUR CONTENT
INTRODUCING CONTENT PRIMER
THE PROBLEM WE ALL FACE
BUT WHAT ABOUT LEGIT REFUND REQUESTS?
DESIGNED TO WORK WITH WSO PRO
HOW DOES IT WORK?
1. CREATE YOUR CONTENT:
2. FILL IN OUR EASY SETUP FORM:
3. Launch your WSO:
LOCK DOWN YOUR CONTENT ONCE AND FOR ALL
ONE APP FOR ALL PRODUCTS
EASY ACCESS FOR USERS
WATCH BRAD GOSSE DEMONSTRATE HOW EASY CONTENT PRIMER IS TO USE
IT'S TIME WE START CHANGING THE WAY WE DISTRIBUTE OUR PRODUCTS
KEEP READING TO LEARN MORE
CUSTOMER SUPPORT DONE FOR YOU
UPDATE ON THE FLY
FINALLY STOP PEOPLE FROM LEACHING YOUR VALUABLE CONTENT
HAS THIS EVER HAPPENED TO YOU?
YOU OWE IT TO YOUR CUSTOMERS TO MAINTAIN THE VALUE OF YOUR PRODUCTS
NO MORE VIDEO PLAYER OR HOW TO UNZIP SUPPORT REQUESTS
FREQUENTLY ASKED QUESTIONS
WE WILL LAUNCH THIS TO THE PUBLIC FOR $97/YR BUT YOU GET A LIFETIME UNLIMITED PRODUCT LICENSE FOR JUST:
BETA TEST GROUP OFFER
YOUR PRICE $27
SPACES ARE VERY LIMITED
CLICK HERE TO ORDER NOW

# CHRONIC MARKETER WHITE PAPERS

This report will outline the 15 things you need to do to make your blog successful. They are all easy to set up and implement and even if you are brand new you should have no problems getting them all done.

By taking the time to set your blog up correctly you will see results faster. So remember to think what purpose your blog is going to serve. Whether it is a branding site, an affiliate site or a site where you will be offering a service. Once you have this decided you can start to set your blog up accordingly.

## GETTING STARTED

If setting up your blog seems overwhelming to you, take small steps. Do a little each day and you will still have your blog set up in ten days or less. Once set up then all you need to do is add content and update when necessary.

If you choose to use a WordPress blog then you will be notified when your site needs to be updated to the new version of WordPress. In my experience I have always found that updating your plugins before doing the WordPress update works better.

To be on the safe side you can always install a WordPress backup plugin. This updates and saves a copy of your site on a regular basis. This way if something ever goes wrong you have a copy of your site backed up.

## #1 SETTING UP YOUR BLOG

The very first step is to actually set up your blog. There are basically two ways that you can go about this and they are paid or free. Now before you choose you want to consider what the purpose of your blog is. Is this a personal blog, an affiliate blog or a blog which you intend to become an authority site?

Now there is nothing wrong with setting up a free blog. What you do want to consider is that if you want your site to become an authority site and make you money then free is not always your best option.

The problem with a free blog is that you have no control over it. It is very possible that your blog could suddenly disappear into hyper space never to return. All your hard work is lost and you will have to start from scratch. This is just a possibility and is something that has happened to many people.

So if you value your blog and want to create something lasting then a paid blog might be your best choice. Having your own blog on your own domain name is not as expensive as you might think. Purchasing a domain name will run you about $10 and monthly hosting can cost as little as $5.

The following are my recommended resources if you would like to look at your options.

**CONTINUED**

The Chronic Marketer white papers are designed to help you live the Chronic Marketer lifestyle. That means being a high functioning entrepreneur. And enjoying life to the fullest by creating businesses that work for us. So we can have fun :)

**MASTERING BLOGGING 101** — SHARE THE LOVE

## #1 CONTINUED

Domain Name Register - GoDaddy

Web Hosting - Certified Hosting

One of the most popular blogging platforms is WordPress. It is a one click installation and can be customized quite easily. You can choose from thousands of templates and themes or you can purchase a customized theme if you prefer.

Installing WordPress on your hosting is very easy. Try to choose a hosting company that uses CPanel. All you do is click on the Fantastico Icon and follow the instructions to get your blog up and running. Just remember to choose the option to email your user name and password to yourself.

### CHOOSING A DOMAIN NAME

If you decide to go this route then you need to get a domain name that reflects what your site is about. If your are attempting to brand yourself as a marketer, freelancer or graphic artist etc, then using your own name is a good choice.

If your blog is about a local service then getting a domain name with your location in will help your rankings in the search engines. If your blog is about dogs get something that matches your main theme or topic as closely as possible. Don't have a name such as World of Dogs, be more specific and choose Labrador Puppies or How to Choose your New Labrador Puppy.

## #2 ORGANIZING YOUR BLOG

Once your blog is installed you need to take some time to think about how to organize it correctly. One vitally important aspect is to keep your reader in mind. You must make it easy for the visitor to find the information they are looking for and quickly! Remember when someone lands on your blog if they don't find what they want they will leave as fast as they arrived.

### DASHBOARD SETTINGS

In this area of your blog you want to configure your settings correctly. In your dashboard area go to settings and then select General. Here you want to add a good blog title and tag line. This is what will show up in the search engines so give it some thought. Try to get your main keyword in the title if possible.

If you wish to make your blog static then you would change these settings in the Reading tab.

Under the Privacy tab make sure that the box which says "I would like my blog to be visible to everyone, including the search engines…" is checked. For some reason the default is the block search engine box. So be certain to change this or no one will find your site.

Permalink Structure – It is important to have your permalinks look professional. This can easily be done by going to settings in your dashboard. Then click on Permalink and then go to the custom box at the bottom.

Once there copy the following link into the box:

/%post_id%/%postname%/

The resulting URL would look something like this:

http://www.yourdomainname.com/715/how-to-start-a-blog/

The Chronic Marketer white papers are designed to help you live the Chronic Marketer lifestyle. That means being a high functioning entrepreneur. And enjoying life to the fullest by creating businesses that work for us. So we can have fun :)

**MASTERING BLOGGING 101** — SHARE THE LOVE

# BASIC ELEMENTS OF A BLOG

The basics that you should have on your blog are:

★ **Homepage** – this is the page where your visitor will arrive. This could be your latest blog post or a static page.

★ **About page** – give your reader some background information about yourself and your aim for your blog. Be sure to include call to action on this page. Whether it is signing up for your RSS feed or newsletter.

★ **Contact page** – provide the visitor with some way to contact you if they have a question

★ **Privacy page** – create your own or use our recommended plugin (found at end of guide)

# CATEGORIES AND TAGS

Think about what categories you want to have on your blog before you get going. This is where you want to stay organized. Your focus should be on making it easy for your visitors to find information. If they have to start looking through too many categories they are likely to get fed up and leave your site.

Tags are another way that the search engines find you, so be sure to add tags to all your posts.

# #3 BLOGGING FREQUENCY

By blogging on a regular basis your site will get indexed by Google faster and you will start attracting more visitors. Before you decide to go ahead and post every day, think about how often you can manage to create posts. Posting three to four times a week is a good goal to have for the beginner.

You should even go as far as working out which days of the week you want to blog on and then stick to your schedule. An easy way to remind yourself is to add the task to your online calendar. Then you will receive a reminder each day when it is time to create a new post.

Many bloggers go as far as creating themes or topics for each day of the week as well. So if you were to blog on a Monday then your theme could be Marketing Tips. For a Wednesday it could be Creating Content and so on.

If time is an issue then you can set your posts to publish on a schedule. This allows you to spend a couple of hours creating content and then setting it to publish three or four times during the week. You can set posts to publish months in advance if you wish. This is also something that could be outsourced to someone if time really is an issue for you.

---

The Chronic Marketer white papers are designed to help you live the Chronic Marketer lifestyle. That means being a high functioning entrepreneur. And enjoying life to the fullest by creating businesses that work for us. So we can have fun :)

**MASTERING BLOGGING 101** — SHARE THE LOVE

# #4 RELEVANT CONTENT

Now that you know which days you will be creating your blog posts you need to think about what you are going to write. It is very important to provide information that matches the topic of your blog. Stay on topic and provide your readers with value. This way they are more likely to sign up for your list and to return time and time again.

Let's say that your site is about dogs, don't start adding content that goes over into general pets, cats and fish. Talk about dogs and provide resource links and other important and useful information.

When it comes to writing content for you blog you need to consider keywords. This is how your site will be found by the search engines. Follow the principle of one keyword per blog post.

Be sure to use the keyword in your blog title, then again in the first sentence or paragraph. Then sprinkle your keyword two or three times throughout your post and use again in the closing of your blog post.

Every blog post needs to have a call to action. This means telling the reader what to do next. If you are offering a free report tell them how to download it, even if the box is underneath tell them in words what to do!

Use your keyword as a hyperlink in your call to action.

Grab Your Free Report on How to Cure Acne Today. If your keywords used to be cure acne this is how you would write your hyperlink:

`<a href="www.yourdomain.com>How to Cure Acne</a>`

These hyperlinks don't always have to point to a sales page or outside link. If your blog contains other relevant information on the same topic, link to it to provide your reader with even more great content.

As well in your blog post you should use bold, italics or underlining to emphasis one or two of your keywords. This shows the search engine spiders that these words are important.

Another great idea to help you with content for your blog is to accept guest posts. This can be an extremely helpful way to drive additional traffic to your site. If you decide to accept guest posts make sure that they are at least 500 words long and have not been published anywhere else before.

Writing blog posts can be difficult, it is very possible to run out of ideas of what to write about. One way to get around this is by using PLR content. PLR is private label rights content which gives you certain rights to use the material in any way you see fit. Normally you are not allowed to resell the content as PLR again.

PLR content is relatively cheap, you can purchase 5 articles for around $5. Then all you have to do is rewrite the content for your blog. You can do this by splitting each article into smaller chunks. Or you could combine them into an e course, short report or turn them into a video or pod cast. All of these methods will provide you with many ways to create tons of new content.

Each article pack you purchase can be reused many times and is also a great way to get your own creative juices flowing.

---

The Chronic Marketer white papers are designed to help you live the Chronic Marketer lifestyle. That means being a high functioning entrepreneur. And enjoying life to the fullest by creating businesses that work for us. So we can have fun :)

**MASTERING BLOGGING 101** — SHARE THE LOVE

# #5 WRITE GREAT HEADLINES

Writing great headlines will first of all attract your visitor's attention, plus it will compel them to read your blog post or article. Your aim is to get your reader to read the entire post. This means making each individual sentence compelling, drawing the reader to the end of your post.

Here's a great tip when trying to come up with great headlines. Do your keyword research and look for long tail keywords that are specific to your niche. These type of keywords will bring you targeted traffic. You may not get as much traffic, but you will have quality visitors. After all, these are the ones that you want. They are more likely to end up subscribing to your list or purchasing your product.

If you perceive keywords as the language of Google, then you are on the right track!
Here are some great ideas to get you started with writing great headlines.

★The Secrets of.....
★Little Known Ways to.....
★What You Should Know about....
★Top Ten Reasons to...
★Here's an Easy Way to....
★The Quickest Way to....

If your blog post is news worthy then create headlines which emphasize this.

★My Exclusive Interview with...
★Breaking News about.....

By making your headline relevant to your post your readers know immediately what to expect. If you are attempting to get subscribers to your list then let them know in the headline.

★Subscribe to....Today!

Many writers advocate creating your own swipe file for writing great headlines. All you do is copy headlines which attract your attention and save them into a file. Then when you are ready to write you simply read through this list and adapt a headline to suit your blog post.

---

The Chronic Marketer white papers are designed to help you live the Chronic Marketer lifestyle. That means being a high functioning entrepreneur. And enjoying life to the fullest by creating businesses that work for us. So we can have fun :)

**MASTERING BLOGGING 101**

SHARE THE LOVE

---

# #6 TARGET YOUR MARKET

When considering what content you are placing on your blog you need to research just who your visitors are. This can be done by going to the following sites and doing some basic research:

★http://quantcast.com/
★http://alexa.com
★http://www.google.com/trends

With these sites you can find out information on the demographics of who your visitors are. If your site is new you simply want to type in the URL of a site that is your competition. This will give you all the basic information you need. So for example if you find out that your site will be visited by males who are in their twenties, then you know how to style your writing. You would write differently than if you were writing for retired couples.

# #7 SOCIAL NETWORKING

To really succeed with your blog today you should be taking advantage of social networking sites. This includes using Facebook, Twitter, LinkedIn to name just a few. If Facebook were a country it would be the third largest country in the world. So if you are not using this you are missing out on a lot of potential traffic and customers!

Your first step is to create accounts and set up a profile at these sites. When using Facebook you are able to create a fan page for your business. This is a good option if you want to keep your professional and personal dealings separate. Fan pages also allow you to promote more than one business, so if you are in different niches then this is a fantastic marketing opportunity for you.

LinkedIn is good to use if you are offering a professional service such as freelancing, web design and graphics and for local businesses. Again it is simply a matter of creating an account and adding all your relevant details.

Adding links to your website will automatically update your account and show your recent activity. You can add business associates and new contacts into your account and this increases your online visibility.

For marketing locally you want to use meetup.com this is another good way to connect with local people in your market. This can allow you to network with others as well as find new clients and customers.

---

The Chronic Marketer white papers are designed to help you live the Chronic Marketer lifestyle. That means being a high functioning entrepreneur. And enjoying life to the fullest by creating businesses that work for us. So we can have fun :)

**MASTERING BLOGGING 101**

SHARE THE LOVE

## TOP SOCIAL BOOKMARKING WEBSITES

The top social bookmarking sites are:

- ★ Twitter
- ★ Stumbleupon
- ★ Reddit
- ★ DeL.icio.us
- ★ Mixx
- ★ Slashdot
- ★ Friendfeed
- ★ Blinklist

You want to use these sites in conjunction with your blog in two ways. First, each time you have published a post you want to submit the link to each site. Secondly, install a social plugin on your site that allows your readers to write comments at these sites. A popular plugin to use is Social Bookmarks for WordPress and this can be done by searching in the plugins section of your dashboard.

Enabling this type of plugin allows your site to get more exposure and attention. Plus of course this activity will be viewed well in the eyes of the search engines, and help your site move up in the rankings.

Your readers will appreciate your blog posts and bookmark them in return, this is a sure sign that your blog is doing well!

## #8 LIST BUILDING WITH YOUR BLOG

If you are not attempting to use your blog to build a list of subscribers, you are essentially flushing money down the toilet. Having a list of people who want more information from you is one way to easily create extra money. In addition by providing your subscribers with useful information you are helping to brand yourself in your market.

To build a list you need to create an opt-in form and this can be done by using an Autoresponder service such as MailChimp. This Autoresponder service will have opt-in boxes which you can easily place on your website or blog.

To get someone to part with their name and email address you have to offer something in return. Depending upon your site this can be a weekly or monthly newsletter, a free report, a discount or coupon to their first purchase or free software.

Making your opt-in form visible is an absolute necessity! Your box or form should show up as soon as your page loads in the visitor's browser. This is termed as showing above the fold. This simply means that your visitor does not have to scroll to see the box.

By being visible right away and by having an offer to tempt them, they are more likely to sign up to your list. One thing to remember here is once they have signed up o not blast a ton of promotional emails at them.

Your first email should be a simple thank you for subscribing to my list and the link to their free product or gift. If you are lost as to what to give them think about using some PLR material too quickly and easily create an ebook or report.

Send an email about every 3-4 days and let your readers get to know you and your business. Then once you have established trust you can start recommending products and other resources to them. Be certain that you have tried these products as your reputation is depending upon this. If you recommend something that turns out to be crappy, your subscribers will hit the unsubscribe button FAST!

Eventually you will have a list of followers who trust you and will purchase your products and refer you to others. This all takes time and effort, but by being consistent you can achieve great results.

---

The Chronic Marketer white papers are designed to help you live the Chronic Marketer lifestyle. That means being a high functioning entrepreneur. And enjoying life to the fullest by creating businesses that work for us. So we can have fun :)

## MASTERING BLOGGING 101
SHARE THE LOVE

---

## #9 ADVERTISING ON YOUR BLOG

One thing that you want to avoid on your blog at all costs is over advertising. If your blog is full of nothing but advertisements for products then your visitors will not stay. Too many choices are actually a bad thing.

If you are attempting to build a list, have an opt-in form and nothing else on your landing page. This gives those two choices, sign up for your offer or leave. You have a 50/50 chance of attracting a new subscriber.

When you do have ads on your blog be certain that they are relevant to your blog. If your blog is about dog food, advertise a dog food product or brand. Don't have an advertisement about getting backlinks to your website. This is just another turn off and a great way to lose visitors.

## #10 USE VIDEOS AND IMAGES

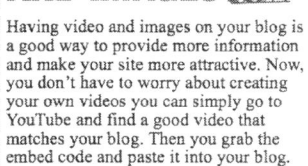

Having video and images on your blog is a good way to provide more information and make your site more attractive. Now, you don't have to worry about creating your own videos you can simply go to YouTube and find a good video that matches your blog. Then you grab the embed code and paste it into your blog.

To center your video on your post use this code <div style="text-align:center"> before the embed code, and this code </div> at the end; this will center your video correctly.

If you are promoting a product with your video you can embed your affiliate link into the video by using one of the following services:

★http://linkedtube.com
★http://viewbix.com

Follow the instructions and your code will be embedded into your video.

A popular option on many blogs today is to record your blog post. This way your readers have the option of listening to you or reading the text version. If you don't want to appear on camera simply use a photo or create a few PowerPoint slides and turn into a video. Or simply record a podcast and upload that to your site.

When using images you can purchase images from photo sharing sites or find free ones to use. When going with the free option you may have to credit the creator of the image or graphic. There are many free photo sites and you can find these by doing a quick online search.

Some of the popular image sites are flicker, photobucket, istockphoto and dreamstime. You will need to create an account and then read the terms and conditions before using.

Another idea is to search for photos and images which are known as public domain, this means that they are free to use and don't require any links.

---

The Chronic Marketer white papers are designed to help you live the Chronic Marketer lifestyle. That means being a high functioning entrepreneur. And enjoying life to the fullest by creating businesses that work for us. So we can have fun :)

## MASTERING BLOGGING 101
SHARE THE LOVE

# #11 RSS FEEDS

RSS stands for Real Simple Syndication and is an extremely good method of getting traffic to your site. It also allows people to subscribe to your feed and be notified each time you create a new piece of content on your blog.

This content must be read through an RSS Reader and Yahoo, Google, AOL and MSN all have their own readers which you can sign up to.

To enable this on your blog you must sign up for an account such as feedburner. You create your account and then follow the instructions, are sure to select the best category possible for your blog.

You will end up with a feed address which will look like this:

http://www.mysite.com/feed.xml

To promote your feed you want to submit it to sites such as feedage.com and feedest.com.

# PINGING YOUR SITE

Another good thing to help your site get exposure is to ping your posts. This can be done at sites such as pingomatic.com. One word of caution here is to not excessively ping your site as this can cause you to get banned from using these types of sites.

# #12 BLOG COMMENTING

Blog commenting is a great way to have interaction on your blog. You want to encourage a person to leave comments and even advice that is helpful to all your readers.

When someone leaves a comment on your blog you want to respond to it and thank them for taking the time to write comments.

It is important to get comments on your own blog, but remember that you are trying to build up your reputation in your niche. One way to do this is by going out and leaving helpful comments on other people's blogs.

Leaving comments is going to provide you with links to your blog and will attract more visitors to your blog. Try to leave comments that are useful but also ones that want the reader to find out more.

A great way to find blogs to post on is by setting up a Google Alert. This service will inform you whenever new posts are published on your particular service. You can include website URL's or keywords to the alert.

The Chronic Marketer white papers are designed to help you live the Chronic Marketer lifestyle. That means being a high functioning entrepreneur. And enjoying life to the fullest by creating businesses that work for us. So we can have fun :)

## MASTERING BLOGGING 101 — SHARE THE LOVE

# #13 GUEST BLOGGING

Guest blogging is a powerful method of getting your name out into your market. Many internet marketers are open to publishing guest posts. They will have information on how to submit your post for consideration directly on their blog. They may even have a list of topics they would like covered.

Before asking to be a guest blogger be sure to read the blog in question thoroughly. This way you can see what type of content is normally published and the average word length of each guest post.

Guest blogging is perfect for any business no matter how large or small. It is great for small local business. It would be easy to create a how to type of post that addresses a common problem. The guest post would end with a solution and how to find it.

Guest blogging can provide you with a lot of satisfaction, especially if you can get published on a large blog. Just imagine sharing your knowledge and helping others improve their life, what could be more satisfying than that?

In addition to this your name gets associated with that of the larger blog or marketer and immediately makes you more of an authority.

Another major benefit of guest blogging is that you are normally allowed to link back to your website. This is where providing a solution or more information comes in useful. If your guest posts links back to your website you can easily get more subscribers to your list.

Just offer the solution in the form of a free report in exchange for their name and email address. This can really be a huge source of list building for you if done correctly.

# #14 LINKING TO OTHER BLOGS

By linking to other blogs with relevant information you are providing additional resources for your readers. These resource links will normally link out to your competitor's sites and by doing this you are providing more information. Plus Google will see you linking to a relevant site and reward you for it.

Linking provides you with trackbacks and this gives you a link to that site from your blog. It is also a smart way to get attention. By linking and referencing another blog, you will attract the attention of the blog owner. They might visit your blog and if they like what they see leave a comment or reference of their own.

If you think of linking as a way to becoming popular you are on the right track. Don't think that you are sending your competition visitors.

One way to find blogs to link on is by subscribing to blogs that interest you in your niche. This way you will be among the first to know when a new post is published. You can then visit this site and leave a comment or reference the link in your own blog post.

Remember being at the top of the comment list normally gets you more exposure, than being down at number 99. Subscribe via email or by the blog's RSS feed.

Many bloggers like to use their blog roll to link out to other blogs they like. This blog roll is recommending other blogs that you think your readers will like.

Hopefully the blog which you are linking to will return the favor and link back to you, but this doesn't always happen.

If you do decide to use the Blog Roll feature on your blog, periodically check that the links are still functioning. It is not good to have dead links on your blog at all.

The Chronic Marketer white papers are designed to help you live the Chronic Marketer lifestyle. That means being a high functioning entrepreneur. And enjoying life to the fullest by creating businesses that work for us. So we can have fun :)

## MASTERING BLOGGING 101 — SHARE THE LOVE

# #15 DO INTERVIEWS

If your content stream runs dry then why not do some interviews? Most marketers will happily do an interview and this can be in the form of an email questionnaire or a Skype call. If done via a call you can post the transcript on your blog and make an audio file available as well.

One advantage of doing an interview with someone is that the person interviewed will gladly promote your blog to their friends and colleagues. This gets you more exposure for your blog and possibly new readers and list subscribers.

It never hurts to approach anyone about being interviewed. Simply ask! Just send the person an email and ask if they are open to being interviewed. Then ask which format they would prefer, email, telephone or via a chat room.

Many marketers today make it a point to make them more accessible and post interview information directly on their blog.

Be prepared for the interview by making a list of questions ahead of time. One tip is to ask the person to come up with one question they wished they would be asked. Maybe they want to give a little insight into a different aspect of their business.

It is also a great idea to ask for a photo shot of the person. This could either be the standard head shot or you might want to request a photo of them being more relaxed. This can work well and allows the reader to connect with the person on a more down to earth basis.

By doing interviews you are getting your name out into your niche and have the opportunity to learn from other marketers.

The following are some sample questions which you can use to get started with your first interview.

★ What are the biggest benefits that your product/service provides to your customers/clients.?

★ What are the most frequent questions you are asked?

★ What would you say is your best kept secret and why?

★ If you could only share one tip with my readers what would that be?

★ When things aren't going well in your business, what do you do to stay positive?

Your goal is to make your interview different and you can do this by trying to squeeze out more personal business information from them. Having an answer to "What was the most difficult business decision you ever had to make?" Is much better than asking, "How did you get started?" This question has probably been asked many times and is well known all over the internet.

---

The Chronic Marketer white papers are designed to help you live the Chronic Marketer lifestyle. That means being a high functioning entrepreneur. And enjoying life to the fullest by creating businesses that work for us. So we can have fun :)

# RECOMMENDED PLUGINS

★ All In One SEO Pack – allows you to set keywords for your home page and each post

★ Google XML Site Map – creates a site map of your blog which allows the search engine spiders to easily crawl your site

★ Google Analytics for WordPress – keeps track of your stats

★ WP Super Cache – allows for fast loading of your blog

★ Sociable for WordPress – allows readers to bookmark posts

★ Follow Me – allows people to follow you on twitter

★ Contact Form 7 – provides a way for someone to contact you

★ Easy Privacy Policy – makes sure your site conforms to Google's requirements

Of course there are many other plugins that can be useful, you can do a quick search in the plugin area for any others that you might need.

# FINAL THOUGHTS

Hopefully you have found these tips invaluable and remember they will only be effective if you take action immediately. By incorporating these tips into your blog you will quickly start to see a difference in your blog's ratings.

The competition on the internet is fierce today and one way to get yourself noticed is by having a blog which stands out above the rest. By posting insightful information your posts and blog itself will start to rise in the search engine rankings. The end result is that you will have a great blog which people are clamouring to read.

To your success!
Chronic Marketer

---

The Chronic Marketer white papers are designed to help you live the Chronic Marketer lifestyle. That means being a high functioning entrepreneur. And enjoying life to the fullest by creating businesses that work for us. So we can have fun :)

# CHRONIC MARKETER WHITE PAPERS

Affiliate marketing means promoting someone else's products. This is the main reason why affiliate marketing is so appealing to the beginner. You don't have to worry about creating your own products. You just choose certain products to promote, grab an affiliate link and you are ready to start making money!

Just take the time to learn the basics of affiliate marketing first. Once you have a good grasp of this then you are ready to take your business to the next level.

Enjoy and happy marketing!

# GETTING STARTED

One of the first things you want to think about when getting started with affiliate marketing is your reputation! You are going to be recommending products to other people. If you recommend crap then people are not going to come back and visit your other suggestions.

You really need to choose your products wisely. Take the time to research the products and the reputation behind the company. Don't worry, you are not going to have to start purchasing all kinds of products. You can read reviews and testimonials and come to your own conclusions.

The basics steps that you are going to go through include:
Setting up your own website – not required but recommended for best results

★ Choosing affiliate companies to promote
★ Choosing a niche
★ Narrowing down your selection of products
★ Promoting your products
★ Using keywords to promote your product
★ Writing product reviews
★ Driving traffic to your site
★ Creating a subscriber list
★ Getting Paid

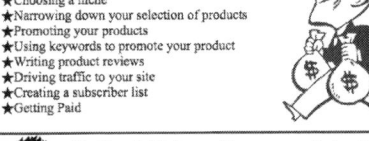

# WHAT IS AFFILIATE MARKETING

An affiliate program is put in place by the owner of a product. This could be an eBook, video series or a line of products. You have probably heard of Clickbank and Amazon, you may have even purchased products there yourself. Well these are large businesses that have put an affiliate program in place.

What this means is that they encourage people to sign up as an affiliate. Then you go out and promote these products. When you get sales the company will pay you a percentage of the money. This could be as little as 5% or as high as 75% or more. Basically you are a sales person working on a commission basis.

This is a very simple concept which is why affiliate marketing holds such an appeal to individuals wanting to make money online. But of course there is a learning curve that needs to be done.

As an affiliate marketer your main objective is to drum up traffic to your affiliate links. Your link takes the prospective buyer straight to a sales page where the company takes over. From here it is up to their sales copy to sell the buyer and make them click on the Buy Now button.

Your goal is to send targeted buyers to these sales pages as then your conversions will be higher. This equals more money in your bank account.

The Chronic Marketer white papers are designed to help you live the Chronic Marketer lifestyle. That means being a high functioning entrepreneur. And enjoying life to the fullest by creating businesses that work for us. So we can have fun :)

# AFFILIATE MARKETING 101 — SHARE THE LOVE

## SO WHAT ARE THE BENEFITS OF BEING AN AFFILIATE?

★ No products to create
★ No inventory to store or purchase
★ No sales copy to write
★ No initial investment
★ Market Worldwide
★ Unlimited income potential
★ Low Risk
★ Promotional material usually provided
★ No deadlines to meet

## CREATING YOUR ACCOUNT

Once you have decided which affiliate company or product you are going to promote then you will need to create an account. Approval time varies depending upon the company. You could be approved immediately or you may have to wait a couple of days.

Note: Some companies require that you have a website or blog before they will accept you as an affiliate. So you may wish to do this step first.

## CHOOSING A NICHE

Before you do anything you want to sit down and choose a niche to promote. The biggest money makers online are those to do with money, relationships and life. This includes niches such as:

★ Make money online
★ Work from home
★ Dating
★ Weight loss
★ Skin care
★ And the list goes on....

Now these are referred to as broad topics. You can categorize many sub categories under these main topic headings. For example let's take a look at the skin care topic. You might find the following subs: Eczema, Psoriasis, Anti aging, Acne, Dry skin, Wrinkles, Warts , Blackheads.

These topics are known as sub niches and the great thing about these niches is that there is less competition in them. This means you can get your pages to rank higher in the search engines so people will find your link and purchase from you.

Your next step is to head over to the Google Keyword Tool and put in these terms. Take a look at the results and make note if there are any Ad words on the right side of the screen. These are paid promotions and are a good indication that people are making money with this niche.

Also look at the number of searches returned by Google you want to target something that has around 50,000 searches per month. As you gain experience you can target higher amounts but remember we want to keep things simple!

For now you want to pick one of these sub niches and start to promote it. In time you can add additional niches and products. But for now it is best to start with one and work your way up.

The Chronic Marketer white papers are designed to help you live the Chronic Marketer lifestyle. That means being a high functioning entrepreneur. And enjoying life to the fullest by creating businesses that work for us. So we can have fun :)

# AFFILIATE MARKETING 101 — SHARE THE LOVE

# CHOOSING YOUR AFFILIATE PROGRAM

There are literally hundreds if not thousands of affiliate programs to choose from. As a beginner it is probably best to start off with one of the more well known companies. These would be Amazon, Clickbank, Commission Junction and Linkshare.

When choosing which program to sign up with you want to take a few things into consideration.

★Check that they take affiliates from your country.
★Find out what payment method they use, check or PayPal are the most common.
★How often do they pay?
★Is there an earnings cap?
★Commission %

These are all important points that are worth a little extra explaining. Some companies like Amazon are now having restrictions placed on where they can do business. For instance people in California, Colorado and Illinois cannot do business with Amazon.

The majority of affiliate programs pay out via check, direct deposit to certain countries or through PayPal. Check to see if you can receive money to your country with these methods. PayPal is adding more countries to their list but there are some restrictions. Note: If you don't have a PayPal account now is the time to set one up and get it verified.

The frequency of your commission payments will vary. Some programs pay out immediately while others can take up to a month or more. Clickbank for instance pays out once every two weeks. It is important to check this so you will understand why you haven't received a commission check yet.

Many affiliate programs put a minimum requirement on your earnings. What this means is that you will not receive payments until certain conditions are met. These normally are:

★Certain number of sales achieved
★Certain cash number required often $50 - $100

Before signing up to promote a product you want to know what percentage you will make on a sale. Is it 5% or 75%? This will make a big difference on your cheque. Look at the price of the product and then determine what your commission would be. If you are happy with this amount then go ahead and sign up as an affiliate.

Some programs like Amazon will pay you for whatever product someone buys from your link. For example say you are promoting a book on skin care the person goes from your link to the gardening sections and buys gardening tools. You will still get the commission. So in essence you are promoting every product in the Amazon store! This could end up netting you a large income.

You can also join affiliate marketing forums and ask questions about what the best affiliate programs to join are. This way you can get feedback and suggestions on who to go with and which products to promote.

---

The Chronic Marketer white papers are designed to help you live the Chronic Marketer lifestyle. That means being a high functioning entrepreneur. And enjoying life to the fullest by creating businesses that work for us. So we can have fun :)

**AFFILIATE MARKETING 101** — SHARE THE LOVE

---

# SETTING UP YOUR OWN WEBSITE

Now there are two different ways to go about this. One is a free method and the other a paid method. It is totally up to you which way you go. The downside to a free method is that you run the risk of losing your website overnight. The free service provider might suddenly decide to delete a whole bunch of blogs or websites for no apparent reason. Your hard work is gone and you will have to start again.

To set up a free blog you can use any of the following sites.

★Blogger
★Hub pages
★Squidoo
★Tumblr

You then register and create your account. A couple of things to remember here are to try and get your sub niche keyword in the title. For instance if you have decided to promote skin care and have narrowed down the niche to psoriasis, then use this word in the name of your site.

If you created an account at blogger.com the name of your blog would look something like this: http://psoriasissymptoms.blogspot.com/ or http://treatingscalppsoriasis.blogspot.com

This one step will allow your blog to be indexed in the search engine that much faster.

Next you want to add content to your site. Aim for 3 to 5 blog posts or short articles. You can write these articles yourself or purchase some private label rights (PLR) articles to use. This latter method is fastest and you can find quality PLR at a reasonable price.

If you choose to write the articles visit some article directories and read a few articles on your subject. Make notes, but do not copy! Then create your own informative articles.

No matter which way you move forward you will want to use keywords in your articles to promote your pages.

## TIPS: CREATING POSTS/PAGES

As well as the articles try to use some photos that relate to your subject on your site. You can find free photos by doing a quick search on the internet.

At the end of each page you want to have a link that contains your affiliate link and takes the reader to the sales page. This can be done by using this code:

`<a href="your affiliate link here"> keyword here</a>`

Some blogging platforms will add this automatically while you are creating the post.

If you haven't gotten your affiliate link yet, apply to the program of your choice and go back into each post or page and add your link.

Note: When creating content for your site keep in mind that you have two types of visitors. The human that you need to connect with and the search engines spiders, which you need to keep happy so your site gets ranked higher.

# KEYWORD RESEARCH

This could actually turn into a whole report by itself. But we are going to go over the basics so you can get content on your site quickly.
Go back to the Google keyword tool and put in your sub niche keyword.

Let's use psoriasis as our example.
Put this word as your main keyword and then check the box that says: Only show ideas closely related to my search terms

After you hit search you will get a list of keywords returned. The Global Monthly search results will show you how many searches are done for these terms. If you click the top you can organize this into an ordered list.

Some of the top keywords listed currently are:

★What is psoriasis?
★About psoriasis
★Treatment for psoriasis

Then organize the list to show the least searched terms and you come up with:

★Plaque psoriasis causes
★Treating psoriasis naturally

You should try and use a combination of these words on your website. Do you also see that these keywords suggest article titles or pages? Now you can have 5 pages of content created quickly.

---

The Chronic Marketer white papers are designed to help you live the Chronic Marketer lifestyle. That means being a high functioning entrepreneur. And enjoying life to the fullest by creating businesses that work for us. So we can have fun :)

**AFFILIATE MARKETING 101** — SHARE THE LOVE

# YOUR OWN WEBSITE

If you are serious about affiliate marketing you may wish to get your own domain name along with web hosting. You can easily do this for around $20. There are two ways you could create a site.

You might decide that you would like to make one huge affiliate website and refer and review all types of products. Or you may wish to make lots of small mini sites and promote just one product per site.

Another option is to stay with the Skin care theme as a general site and then have pages specifically aimed at the various sub niches.

Whichever way you go try and get a domain name that has your keyword in it. For a general affiliate site you may wish to use terms such as 'recommended product reviews' or 'today's best picks'.

Once you have purchased a name and a hosting account you can install wordpress and set up your own site following the instructions from above. Now you are ready to start promoting your site.

## GIVE AWAY SOMETHING OF VALUE

This is going to be a sure fire method of getting your affiliate site seen. Give visitors to your site something extra! The easiest way to do this is by providing them with a report. In our example this would be a report on psoriasis and could cover the causes and treatment of psoriasis.

Inside the report you would place your affiliate link so they can still click through to the sales page and make a purchase.

By giving away a free report you are building yourself a mailing list. This gives you the opportunity to promote other products in this niche.

The way to do this is to sign up for an auto responder service. There are free or paid services that you can use. Most of them will have sign up forms that you can install on your site. Then once someone enters their name and email address your report is delivered to them.

# DRIVING TRAFFIC TO YOUR PROMOTION

Now that you have a site set up you need to concentrate on getting traffic to your site. Remember the more people that see what you have to offer the more likely they are to click through and make a purchase.

Most affiliate programs will provide you with marketing material. This includes items such as banners and buttons, pre written emails and articles. This is all helpful material but remember lots of other affiliates will be using the same content.

So how can you make your content stand out above the rest?

Well your best bet as a beginner is to take the material that you are given and change it. This can be done by taking the example articles or emails and then rewriting them a little. Try and make the content directly related to the item that you are promoting. Including facts and figures is a good way to do this or even making comparisons to another product.

If we stay with our psoriasis theme then research the product you are promoting and directly list the benefits on your site. Find some customer testimonials and include those too.

---

The Chronic Marketer white papers are designed to help you live the Chronic Marketer lifestyle. That means being a high functioning entrepreneur. And enjoying life to the fullest by creating businesses that work for us. So we can have fun :)

**AFFILIATE MARKETING 101** — SHARE THE LOVE

---

# MORE TRAFFIC GENERATION METHODS

Your goal now is to get people to visit your site. To do this you have to let people know that you exist. This can be done in many different ways including:

★ Using social media sites
★ Forum posting
★ Guest posts
★ Blog commenting
★ Paid advertising
★ Article writing
★ Directory submissions
★ Video Marketing

To do this effectively, start off by creating a Facebook and Twitter account and posting information about your site there. Try to give people tips, advice and basic facts. Don't do a hard sell. Do a search on Twitter and find people in your niche and follow them.

Find forums in your niche and join them. Then start answering questions and being helpful. Over time you will be seen as someone who knows what they are talking about and people will refer your site to others.

When filling out your forum profile make references to your niche and either a photo of yourself or one related to your niche.

If you see certain questions being repeated then create an article about them and refer people back to your site. Let them know about your free report. Most people are happy to get something for free and will gladly visit your site to pick it up. Check the terms and conditions of the forum and if you are allowed create a link in your signature leading back to your website. You can hyperlink your affiliate link to something like Free Skin Care Report.

Writing additional articles and submitting them to online directories is another way to get traffic back to your site. You can also write an in-depth product review and submit that.

Blog posting and commenting are other great traffic generation ideas. You can find blogs in your niche and leave helpful comments. An easy way to do this is to sign up for Google Alerts and insert your keywords. Then every time a new blog is indexed Google will notify you. You then leave a comment and hopeful it gets approved.

Once your website has lots of content you can offer to write guest posts on other blogs. Just make sure that the content is unique and that you won't publish it anywhere else. This will help you become known as an expert in your niche and give you links back to your site.

You will also want to promote your sites and articles to places like Reddit, Stumbleupon, Jump tags and Delicious. There are many other sites you can use as well.

---

The Chronic Marketer white papers are designed to help you live the Chronic Marketer lifestyle. That means being a high functioning entrepreneur. And enjoying life to the fullest by creating businesses that work for us. So we can have fun :)

**AFFILIATE MARKETING 101** — SHARE THE LOVE

## TRACKING YOUR EFFORTS

A smart affiliate marketer is going to want to track their results. This way you will know if your efforts are paying off. Some affiliate programs have tracking software built into them. If not there is an easy way for you to do this.

All you need to do is install Google Analytics on your wordpress site. This will then track things like your most frequently visited pages and which keywords are being used to find your site.

It is also possible to set your account up to automatically email your stats to you monthly. Then you can see which keywords, pages are getting the most traffic as well as where this traffic is coming from.

With this information all you do is create more content about your most used keyword to drive additional traffic.

The Chronic Marketer white papers are designed to help you live the Chronic Marketer lifestyle. That means being a high functioning entrepreneur. And enjoying life to the fullest by creating businesses that work for us. So we can have fun :)

## FINAL THOUGHTS

When writing content for your affiliate marketing site always keep the following in mind:

You are writing to form a relationship with your reader. By creating trust they will gladly purchase from you time and time again!

The best way to achieve this is to write in a friendly manner as though you are talking to a friend. Be honest about the product you are reviewing. If there is a negative get it out in the open and tell your readers about it.

Use sites like Yahoo Answers to find out what problems people have in your niche. Then write short articles and place them on your site. You can then answer this question by directing people back to your site and your free report.

To really become successful at affiliate marketing you should research who exactly your customer is. If you know exactly what age they are, what their main concerns are you can then address these issues on your site. When your visitor arrives they feel as though you are writing to them personally and they begin to trust you already.

This begins to take you into more advanced areas of affiliate marketing. Right now we have given you the basics to get started on your new career choice.

If you are interested in advanced tactics then these are some of the things you can look forward to learning.

★Cloaking your affiliate links
★Using paid advertising campaigns
★Spying on your competition
★Research your target market
★Creating auto blogs
★Participate in more crowded niches
★Leveraging your email list
★Offering bonuses to your customers
★SEO tactics
★Backlinking

As you can probably see the world of affiliate marketing is huge along with the potential of making a great income. So get started today and start carving out your own place in this lucrative market!

To your success!
Chronic Marketer

## AFFILIATE MARKETING 101

SHARE THE LOVE

# WEBSITE TRAFFIC

# Chapter 11: Website Traffic

The easiest and fastest way to get traffic to your website is to buy it.

Too often I see people trying what they call "bum marketing". In other words writing articles, spinning articles, hiring crappy outsourcers to write articles and posting them to hundreds of useless article websites in the hopes that those websites will create enough link juice to make Google love them one day. What a waste of resources, time and bandwidth.

If you have a product, you need to prove how well it works right away. And if it doesn't, you need to make changes to how it's presented until it sells. The easiest way to do that is by making test traffic purchases. You can buy an almost unlimited amount of traffic from websites like Facebook, Google, advertising networks, e-mail lists and more. Personally, I like to buy traffic from Facebook because I believe they have some of the best targeting in the business. They make it easy for me to find the exact group of people I want to promote my products to.

In fact, when building the list for this book, I purchased traffic from Facebook and only targeted self-confessed potheads. There aren't many other places I could access 5 million of you.

I could've written an entire book on how to buy traffic. There are plenty of courses out there and lots of free information that will show you how to do this. My advice is pretty simple. Buy your traffic first. You will never attract affiliates until you have an offer that sells extremely well. A big mistake I see website creators making, is that they launch their product on an affiliate network day one. They haven't tested it to be successful. Now your affiliates are your guinea pigs. And if your offer has some simple flaw that could have been solved with testing you have now lost your affiliates for life.

Instead, buy your own traffic and make changes to your offer until everything is optimized as much as possible. You need to keep testing until you find the way to spend the least amount of money for the most return. In my experience you can easily turn $1 into $4 buying Facebook traffic. But it won't happen the first time you put a banner up, so be prepared to make changes on the fly.

Something else I've been testing to work extremely well is buying traffic from porn sites to my mainstream offers. Porn websites have some of the cheapest traffic and ad space available. It's a great way to send thousands of people to your offer to see what sticks. Obviously not everything will sell on a porn site. But keep this in mind, everyone who uses toothpaste may not watch porn, but everyone who watches porn uses toothpaste.

Another great source of traffic is e-mail. If your product is complementary to that of a product that is already selling well, you should contact its creator. Many times they will be willing to e-mail their list in exchange for a commission. Again you don't want to make this person your guinea pig. Once your offer is tested, it's easy to approach people with big e-mail lists in your niche. Sometimes you will have to pay, but it can often be worth it. Sometimes it helps to look in unexpected places.

When my wife Claire was launching her cookbook, I approached many vegan website owners about e-mailing their lists. I didn't just approach the blogging community. Although when I did, I came across a social media hippie who owns vegan.com. What an asshole this guy was. Basically telling me he would never promote my product because of the way the sales copy was written. I got a handful of bloggers to review the cookbook and e-mail it to their list. Beyond that I got in touch with a handful of nonprofit organizations that cater to vegans. One of them in particular wanted $200 for me to e-mail their list of 7000 vegan recipe seekers. That single e-mail brought in thousands in sales. Never be afraid to look for organizations with big followings. Often a nonprofit organization will e-mail their entire list or add you to their newsletter for very little in return.

The next few chapters cover a few other traffic generation methods.

# WEBINARS

# Chapter 12: Webinars

Okay so let's say you have some intangible or tangible products you want to sell. One really cool way to get the attention of your list and convert them into high-paying customers is running a webinar.

A webinar is a free presentation where you give away a lot of content and at the end sell them something they need. It's similar to doing a real-world talk except you can show up high and in your underwear :-)

There are plenty of sites like Goto Webinar that offer a platform for you to run webinars. Rather than talk about the technical side of webinars which I'm sure you can figure out on your own, I'm going to talk about how I've run webinars effectively.

The best webinars are ones where you teach people how to do something cool and then offer additional content, tools and resources to make that cool thing even easier. To simplify it with an analogy, imagine teaching people to sew by hand, and then selling them a sewing machine :-)

My webinars follow a pretty simple format. I talk about myself for the first 15 to 20 minutes to establish credibility. Then I will teach something they likely didn't know before which builds instant trust on top of my credibility. Then I asked them if they received value from the webinar and if they mind me showing them a way to hit the ground running with this new knowledge. Inevitably a bunch of people enter the chat and say yes, I learned something, thank you, etc. then I go into my sales pitch which actually comes off a bit like an infomercial but that works.

I tell them what I'm offering, and I establish the value of what that offer is usually in the thousands of dollars. I then do the whole you won't pay $1800 you won't even pay $997 not even $500 and no not even $197. Tonight only I'm going to offer this for the low price of $97. Trust me, the dog and pony show works. It feels funny the first time you do it, but not as funny as a carny feels the first time he says "who wants to win a giant panda?"

I also find it works very well to put a countdown timer at the end for about 15 minutes This allows people time to ask questions about your offer or what you just taught them. Your ability to answer questions in this 15 minutes will directly impact the volume of sales you make. Treat people well, offer good advice and be patient. Remind them often about how awesome your offer is and when the timer is up end the webinar on time.

Then depending on how you structured your offer you might say that the buy link is available until midnight, or maybe you haven't set a time limit at all. Whatever you do make sure you follow through. If you promise to double the price tomorrow morning, double the price tomorrow morning. And if someone e-mails you asking you for last night's price, tell them you are unable to dishonor your promises.

It's very important to train people. They need to understand that when you say you're going to do something, you do it. They will respect you for it even if they cry. The next time they are told your offer is limited, they won't hesitate to jump.

If you don't already have a list of subscribers, often you can run webinars by leveraging other people's lists and offering them an affiliate commission on your backend offers, groups on LinkedIn.com, Facebook ads etc.

Of course make sure you are collecting the registrant's information and putting it on your subscriber list. These people will likely buy from you again in the future.

I can't stress enough how important good content is. I see many people running "webinars" today that have very little content. It goes from about me to about my product to buy my product. Your conversion rate (the ratio of visitors to sales) will always be much lower if you make people sit through an entire sales pitch that has nothing they can take home. The law of reciprocity makes it easy to sell something when people feel like they got value from the last 45 minutes If they feel like they've been jerked around (and everyone has a really good bullshit detector today) they won't buy from you and they'll never come back to another webinar that you put on.

It's also important to be yourself when you run a webinar. I do mine uncensored, complete with dirty jokes, swearing, bong hits and stories about porn. I don't apologize for it, I have an audience that loves it and the people who don't can suck it :-)

# SOCIAL MEDIA

# Chapter 13: Social Media

High school.

That's the first thing I think of when I think about social media. Not many people will explain it to you this way, but it's essentially a giant popularity contest. The cool kids win. What do they win? Traffic, sales, notoriety, and often free stuff from companies trying to get them talking.

Knowing that social media is a popularity contest, it's important to remember the things that make us popular.

When I go to parties, I like to mingle and meet new people. One of the things I try not to do is talk about myself. Unless asked. Instead when I meet new people I like to interview them. This isn't some tactic that I use to make people like me. I really am interested and I ask follow-up questions based on the things they tell me that I find most interesting. Since people love to talk about themselves, they will go on and on. At the end of each conversation people tell me how they loved chatting with me. Because they got to answer my questions :-)

Social media is exactly the same. Ask people for their opinions, how do they like things?

I often hear people say things like "I don't have time for social media." Or my favorite "I can't be bothered to tell the world about my daily minutia like what I had for breakfast this morning"

I remember my friend Justin Popovic was doing a talk. I offered to tag along with him so he would have some photos to use later.

One of the attendees was this old woman walking around on a cane. She approached me during a break and immediately began telling me all kinds of personal things about herself. She told me about why she was walking on a cane, all her various illnesses, and a bunch of other bullshit that I didn't give a fuck about. Being the polite guy that I am, I smiled and nodded my head pretending that I cared.

When Justin started the social media part of his talk, he began mentioning Twitter. The same woman immediately raised her hand and proclaimed she didn't have time for Twitter because she didn't care to hear about other peoples daily lives.

If I was the speaker I would've called her out on her bullshit. But instead I spent a good time of the drive home with Justin laughing at her hypocrisy.

So people DO care about the minutia. They just care more about their OWN than they do yours. That's your advantage. If you want to do well with social profiles on sites like Facebook and Twitter, you need to ask questions.

I will get more responses asking people about their favorite breakfast cereal than I ever will telling them what I had for breakfast. The more you ask questions the more people respond. The more they respond the more popular you become. When you win the popularity contest, you win at social media.

I guarantee you that there will be social media hippies talking about what I say. They will try to tell you that social media is about value, it's about giving back, free love and all that other bullshit. All I know is the more popular you become, the more traffic and sales you get. The key is they have to follow you because they like you not because you used some automated software or service to get more followers.

When you meet someone at a conference, add them to Facebook and Twitter. But don't go adding random strangers unless they are people you want to contact.

Most people think once they get to a certain level of friends and followers they can just start spamming the shit out of them. That's not the case. You need to ask questions all the time, reply when people need help, and yes once in a while drop some links. We're not doing this to save the whales after all, we are here to make money.

Of course make sure you have an awesome profile picture that you use on social media. It should be you and not a picture of your product. The name you use should be your own not your company or your product. Be a real person.

# BLOGGING

# Chapter 14: Blogging

There was a time when blogging was for a few geeks. It comes from the term web log. Which used to be people posting their personal diaries on the Internet.

Today blogging is much more about the management system that delivers content to your website than it is about posting your personal diary, although it can still work for some.

Having a blog is a fantastic way to cultivate your audience. Whether you're posting articles or videos like I do, your credibility grows with each new post. Again it doesn't have to be a personal diary anymore. I use my blog to give business advice, tell stories and sometimes just have a little fun. Each piece of content builds on top of the last. In fact I got many of my chapter ideas for this book by going through my blog archives to see some of the things I talk about.

You have to decide whether you want to have a personally branded blog, a business blog or both.

For me a personally branded blog is plenty. I use it to promote my own brand and my various business properties all from one place. You can learn a lot about me by just watching my blog videos. In fact people often tell me they feel like they already know me after watching some of them.

In order to grow your blog audience, you need to be active in the blog community that matches your niche. Comment on popular blogs, but make sure your comments add value to what's already been said. Every time you comment on another blog you have an opportunity to link back to your blog. People often make the mistake of trying to link back to products they are selling. This will get you flagged for spam almost every time. Instead link your comments back to your personal blog.

Another cool way to help cultivate your blog audience is by guest posting on other blogs. You'd be surprised how many bloggers are hungry for fresh content. Again no shortcuts here, don't try and send the same article to 50 blogs hoping they will all post it. Instead write an article that resonates with that blog audience specifically. But also make sure that your content is true to your own brand. This will help you to find the people who think you are awesome.

Don't try to think of your blog as a platform for making money. I don't know very many bloggers who have been successful as bloggers alone. My blog is an extension of everything else I do, so I can't measure the returns that it gives me because it's part of a holistic effort.

When it comes to creating content for your blog I have a simple strategy. I only create content when I am inspired to do so. Trying to create content on a schedule just means creating crappy content. Instead I wait for a good story to develop within my business or life. My blog has all kinds of content. I discuss everything from search engine optimization to getting suite upgrades at hotels. It's as much about my lifestyle as it is about my business. My friends, family and my customers all visit my blog. I cater to the entire audience.

# SEARCH ENGINE OPTIMIZATION

# Chapter 15: Search Engine Optimization

Since I have been lucky enough to hold the number 1 spot on Google for porn, I figured I should at least include a short chapter on search engine optimization.

Everyone wants to be at the top of Google, but only a select few websites will ever get there. I don't really like search engine optimization as a marketing strategy the way I used to. It still has value and I spend a little bit of time managing it. What I don't do is focus all of my time on this one strategy. Instead I take care of the basics. Things like on page optimization. This stuff is so easy you can Google how to do it. If you're like me you run a WordPress website, download a few search engine optimization plug-ins and you'll be fine. Follow the basic on page stuff.

From there, the bigger job is what we call link building. This is where 90% of the work is done. At the time of writing this book Google still values sites with more inbound links higher than it does anything else. What's changed recently are the type of sites linking to you and the gravity that they have.

Today it means more to get lots of mentions on Twitter and Facebook than it does to have lots of random webpages linking back to you. It's not a game of quantity anymore it's a game of quality which means focusing on this as a strategy is actually a bad business move.

One of the biggest mistakes I see new people in this business making is focusing time, and money on some grand SEO strategy. In some cases it can take years for the strategies to pay off. Many times by the time you hit the end of the road, algorithms change leaving you in the dark once again.

Instead, budget some money for advertising. If you can't turn $1 into $1.20, all the search engine optimization in the world will not help you. Your traffic needs to convert first. Not to mention once you figure out how to turn $1 into a profit you can scale your spending quickly, even borrowing capital if necessary.

Buying traffic from places like Facebook will be a very easy way to increase your search engine notoriety. Make sure you put Facebook like buttons, Twitter buttons etc. on your website to make this easy for your visitors. Social proof is the best SEO strategy I know of.

Stay away from search engine optimization experts. Most of them have no business taking your money. And most don't have a real track record. In my experience it's more lucrative to work on my own sites than doing it for others. Many times companies will cold call you or fill out contact forms on your website offering you are positioning on Google. My advice is to focus your time on buying advertising. Let the broke newbies spend their time link building and spinning their wheels. You have a business to build.

# EMBRACE YOUR LAZINESS

# Chapter 16: Embrace Your Laziness

I'm lazy.

It's a simple fact, I hate working, I especially hate pointless work and manual labor.

It took me a while to figure out that I am lazy. Mainly because my ego didn't want me to admit it. Nobody likes to admit being lazy. But guess what? Admitting you are lazy makes it much easier to embrace your laziness.

When I was in school, they thought perhaps I had a learning disability. The problem was I scored extremely high on tests, but when it came to the everyday work I wasn't interested.

Who knew that not giving a fuck about math could be misconstrued as a learning disability?

You see I understood how to do the work, I just didn't understand why I had to do it repetitively, and why I had to show my work as you do in math. Once I learned how to do something, I didn't need to do it again. It frustrated me so much to do it a second time unnecessarily, that I simply refused.

Of course the public school system is completely designed to teach you to do something and then force you to do it repetitively for years. It's because they are training you to work in a factory and do the same thing over and over again.

Running a business online is probably the easiest thing for someone who is lazy because for the most part once you set up your business and get all wheels turning, you don't really have to do anything repetitively that you don't want to. In fact I outsource all of my repetitive activities to staff today.

Being lazy doesn't mean I spend all day lying on the sofa watching Maury Povich. It means constructing a lifestyle that allows me to not work whenever I choose. As I write this chapter, or I should say as I dictate this chapter using software, I am sick.

I just returned from a trip to Los Angeles where I had to do a talk to several hundred porn industry people. The trip was great, but I caught a cold while I was there (I need to stop french kissing hobos). Today is a Tuesday and I have some stuff on my calendar but I have cleared most of it away. Because I can.

For me, laziness is actually the driver of my productivity. I try to get the most done in the shortest amount of time every day. I also try to ensure that I have set things in motion before I walk away from my desk. This could be everything from making sure employees are busy, setting up software to run, uploading batches of files etc.

I can relax so much more when I know that other people are working.

I will never get involved in a business that requires me to work certain hours. My dad owns a furniture store. He is in his 60s and is still somewhat a slave to retail hours. It was very important to me not to structure my business life this way. My dad is probably one of the hardest working entrepreneurs I know, and he is successful. But I understood early on that working hard and being successful don't necessarily have to go hand-in-hand.

In fact in my business I have learned that the "harder" I work the less productive I become. Early on when times were tough I assumed that spinning my wheels and putting more hours in would result in more revenue. Unfortunately I have a blueprint in my past that proved this philosophy to work.

However I learned that those past successes based on spinning my wheels were actually flukes. They may have happened without me spinning my wheels in fact I'm sure they would have. It took me spinning my wheels to the point of exhaustion before I realized I didn't have the mental bandwidth to take on all the projects I wanted.

As a new entrepreneur it's easy to get caught up in taking on opportunities. We are often afraid that the one opportunity we turn down will be extremely successful and leave us in the dust. There was a time when I said yes to almost every partnership opportunity that came my way.

I burned myself out in the process. When you are successful everyone wants to work with you. What you need to realize is that the most successful people are not only ruthless with their time but extremely picky with their opportunities. As with most good lessons I learned this myself by failing several times.

Here are a few lessons in embracing your laziness.

Don't partner with someone who has a full-time job or business.

My wife Claire and I were visiting a personal trainer every week. This guy was very good at what he did and during my sessions with him would constantly pitch me his Internet business ideas. He wanted to take fitness online which I knew was a huge niche so I took interest. The problem was, I hate fitness. I like being fit, I like the results I get from working out, but I hate the process.

When I was a kid I discovered that by simply forgetting my gym shorts, I didn't have to participate in gym class. So I conveniently forgot my gym shorts every day.

This trainer wanted to start a website doing spin classes online. It all sounded good. He told me he had his own mailing list and could sell hundreds of subscriptions on his own. This also made the deal attractive because I didn't have to feed it with all the traffic myself.

After taking on the project, spending countless hours in video production, design, market research etc. I realized that I had no love for running a fitness website. Even worse, the trainer was unable to get more than three people to join the website.

The project was done, but the business wasn't going anywhere. At this point many people will hold on because they've done all the work, told their friends and family about the website etc. I on the other hand decided to walk away from the project because I realized there would be no payoffs.

The trainer was expecting me to send a flood of sign-ups to his website. I was expecting him to do the same thing. Neither of us was performing and it was time to shut down the partnership.

Because I saw no value, I essentially handed over my half to the trainer. I needed to focus my time on better things. The trainer eventually found another techie person to partner with. And after several years the site still went nowhere.

I like to think of every business I get into as an investment. Even if I'm not investing a dime of my money. My time is just as valuable as my money. If I'm investing time into a project I treat that time just like its money.

Consider this scenario:

I approach you with my business idea, ask you to invest $25,000 in exchange for 50% of the company. I tell you you're going to get your money back plus profits in six months.

Six months later I come to you and tell you that things didn't go according to plan and that I wasn't going to be able to pay back your $25,000. In fact I need another $25,000 from you in order to keep the project afloat. Promising that in six months you will have your $50,000 plus profit.

An emotional investor will quickly throw good money after bad trying to recoup their losses. A wise investor will abandon the project and write the $25,000 off as a loss.

You need to be a wise investor with your time and your money. If a project is going according to plan and you don't see a light at the end of the tunnel, get out.

One of the main reasons why the above business didn't work was because both myself and the personal trainer had other things to focus our time on.

I run several different businesses. Although I always make time for the partnership I commit to, I often prioritize the ones that make me the most money over the ones that are treading water.

The personal trainer however had his full-time personal training business that ate up most of his hours. So we had to work around his training schedule when it came time to produce content. Often we could only meet with him on weekends or evenings because he was busy during the day.

This is a recipe for disaster.

You see people who aren't full-time entrepreneurs, don't have the hunger. Without hunger you lose focus. It's easy to come home from your good paying job and tell yourself you had a hard day so you're not going to work on your side project. Instead you'll be lazy and sit in front of the television. There's nothing wrong with this.

People are often optimistic about their time in the future but when it comes to the present we aren't very optimistic at all. So we often make commitments to projects we think we can do in our "spare time". But then we realized quickly that we don't really have any spare time.

I recently learned this lesson again. I'm getting much better at saying no in advance, but this was a project with someone whom I respect, and it was an idea that I thought was awesome.

One of my good friends approached me with an idea of his two years ago. Without going into too much detail the idea was gold, so I offered to invest early, but my friend was confident he could do everything himself.

Eventually he quit his job to focus on this business full-time. This was a sign to me that he was committed to being an entrepreneur.

After about 10 months of development, he was very close to a finished platform that could be marketed and sold to the public. Unfortunately he got caught up in the minutia. To the point where he decided to go and take a full-time job. I'll never forget yelling at him literally when he told me he took a job. This was the ultimate sign of failure in my world.

A few months later he approached me to take me on as his partner. He had taken the business as far as it could go and needed my help with sales and marketing. I had all the assets in place, a big mailing list, a network of affiliates and the knowledge to launch his business and see if it was going to sink or swim.

Once I came on board I realized very quickly that this was not a finished business. In fact the 10 months of work my friend had done needed to be scrapped. The project was an absolute mess and needed to be started from scratch.

After taking this on for several months, spending money out of my own pocket and time I realized that this business had a long way to go before it would be considered an actual business.

It's never easy to disappoint a friend. Especially when you have love for a project.

I made the hard decision just a few weeks ago and broke the news to my friend that I could no longer be a part of this project. He wasn't happy. I don't even know at this point if our friendship will survive. Hopefully it will, but my sanity comes first.

You see, I could have kept this project on my plate but it wouldn't have left me a lot of free time. My friend has a full-time job that's very demanding. So the only time we could work together was during a 30 minute lunch break that he had each day, the occasional evening and the odd weekend when his wife was out of town. This made getting anything done extremely difficult because unfortunately he needed to be involved in every detail.

By shedding this project, I'm able to spend less time working. This actually helps me to be much better and much more effective when I am working. My best ideas come to me while I am on vacation. There's a reason for this, it's because I'm allowing myself some downtime. I am at my best when I'm well rested.

One of the hardest things to come to terms with is letting go of a project that may end up being successful. In this case I actually hope the project is successful. Because I want all of my friends to have success. I hope this project ends up making my friend millions.

The difference is, I understand that there are plenty of other opportunities for me to make my own money, and that giving up an opportunity that ends up being successful doesn't mean I have lost. It just means that that opportunity was not right for me.

Today I understand more than ever how important my down time is to my overall productivity. Taking vacations, playing Xbox, exercising, meditation etc. used to always carry feelings of guilt for me. I always felt like I should be working while I'm doing these leisure activities. One of the things that helped me shift out of this mindset was just recognizing that feeling guilty wasn't helping at all. Instead I took the attitude that I was entitled to these luxuries. In fact now I know I'm entitled. I will never feel guilty for playing Xbox while everyone else is working. Those people are working because I allow myself the downtime to play Xbox. Without that downtime I wouldn't be creative, and they wouldn't have jobs.

I think I used to picture my employees scheming and hating on me for taking it easy while they worked. And I can tell you for fact some of them did. Luckily today I have a team of people who aren't so petty. They understand the simple fact that without me they wouldn't have a job. And I have put in my share of late nights and weekends along the way. In hindsight I know it wasn't necessary but I did it anyway. Now I'm just smarter about it.

When you give yourself downtime, resist the temptation to check your phone for messages etc. be present in the moment. I sometimes have difficulty with this. I want to check my stats and see if anybody's paid money into my accounts while I've been watching TV. When I should really be engaging my mind in the entertainment on my screen.

Lastly seek out leisurely activities for yourself, don't just wait for them to come along. Go out for walks, schedule hikes, go on spa vacations, or just visit a day spa. I try to get out to my local spa at least once a month for either a facial, manicure or pedicure. It's some of the most relaxing time I give myself and it feels awesome. It's times like this where I come up with my best ideas. Why would I deprive myself of leisure time that actually contributes to increasing my bottom line?

There should be no guilt in that whatsoever.

**FREELANCER   PRODUCER   OVERSEER**

# THE 3 PHASES OF
# ENTREPRENEURSHIP

# Chapter 17: The 3 Phases Of Entrepreneurship

In all my years as an entrepreneur I have witnessed and experienced 3 distinct phases. Although I like to consider them steps on the ladder I also understand the need to jump back and forth between each phase at different times during your career.

I will explain each of the 3 phases in detail.

**The Freelancer**
This is where almost every entrepreneur starts. The freelancer is always busy, looking for clients and servicing those clients. It's as close to being an employee as you can get. The main difference being a little bit more time freedom. The freelancer is constantly selling themselves and looking for business. If you perform any kind of service like web design, consulting, copywriting, writing etc. you fall into this category.

**The Producer**
Every freelancer should strive to become a producer. The producer has figured out how to productize his talents. He knows that there is a quicker path to money as a freelancer but prefers the power of leverage over time. The freelancer won't work until the client gives them a job. The producer creates work to be sold multiple times to multiple clients. As a for instance, a good writer could easily be writing e-books, paperbacks or private label rights books for resale. Slowly producing a catalog of products that will continue to earn a residual income. It's never easy to start out as a producer and if you are a freelancer who needs to make the jump, I suggest

utilizing as much of your spare time as possible to tap your talents.

**The Overseer**

This is where we all want to be. Overseeing a systemized business with people in place to take care of everything. Problems don't flow up to you unless they are on a grand scale. Your only role may be a weekly meeting where you inject leadership into your project. Once you have created a business as a producer, it's very easy to graduate to the overseer. Your catalog of products will eventually earn enough money to pay support staff, hire freelancers to help you produce more products and pay marketing people to buy traffic and find affiliates. As any good entrepreneur, you likely won't sit in this position for very long. I get very bored during my overseer phases and usually end up jumping back into the producer role over and over again.

I can't stress how important it is to see each of these phases as fluid. You may have multiple projects on the go where you play a different role in each one. That's okay. But take a good look at each of these phases and try to choose one that's best for you. Some people absolutely love being a freelancer and working with clients. I'm not that person. So I tend to stick to producer and overseer roles. I would say the most fun role for me is being a producer. I love to create content. I'm doing it right now with this book. When it's done, I will assume a bit more of an overseer role once all the marketing is in place. And of course my A.D.D. will eventually kick in and I will need to start producing something new :-)

# OUTSOURCING & HIRING

# Chapter 18: Outsourcing And Hiring

I've always had people working for me. Even when times are tough, I always maintain a minimum of 1 full-time employee in my business. My view is that if I can't employ one person outside of myself I don't have a business.

The hiring game has changed so much over the years that it's hard to establish time-tested habits. I usually just go with my gut when it comes to hiring. But today we have so many other choices such as whether or not to hire locally or outsource offshore to a country where labor is cheaper.

I believe it's always best to start with local talent. Find someone who you can get together with once in a while. Make them your right hand. They should know everything you know about your job so they can do it for you. Be willing to let go of everything you think you control. This takes time to get used to but it's worth it. I can't tell you how many times I've had to fight the urge to just do something myself because it's faster than sitting down and teaching my assistant, Megan, how to do it. But I'm much better off once I show her how to do something because I never have to do it again.

I pay above-average wages to my local and offshore talent. I believe it's extremely important to compensate people well for the jobs they do. I also believe it's important that they get something I refer to as time freedom. My policy for days off is pretty simple. I don't care if you're sick, or just want the day off to go and have fun. When someone asks me for a day off I say yes. I don't need to know why because I don't believe it to be my business. If they want to tell me that's fine, but it's not necessary. I don't ever want people who work for me to feel like they have to make excuses. Sometimes we just need a day off. I don't have to jump through hoops when I need a day off and I don't want my people to feel like they have to either.

The best part about having someone like Megan as my right hand is that she can hire outsourcers for us to handle the more mundane tasks. So not only does she remove the burden of a workload from me, she also has the power to delegate jobs that she doesn't want to do to our outsourcers.

I use a website called easyoutsource.com to hire my low priced labor. We currently have a full-time virtual assistant and a full-time cartoonist in the Philippines. Each gets paid a few hundred dollars per month full-time. I always pay a little bit more than they ask for and make sure they are always happy.

I wouldn't hire a customer service representative or a writer in the Philippines. In my experience, the time, language and cultural differences make it very difficult for them to understand and communicate in finite detail.

Hiring a cartoonist in the Philippines made sense because drawing skills transcend language. A cartoonist here would want 20x what mine asked for and would produce the same result. Anyone who is doing graphics work, website design or layouts is going to be a good choice for outsourcing.

Working with my cartoonist is simple. Using a free service called dropbox.com I am able to share a folder on my hard drive with my cartoonist. In that folder I maintain a text file with a list of the next things I want her to draw. Sometimes I will give her a folder full of images I want her to make into cartoons. While I am sleeping peacefully in my bed, she is working on 3 or 4 cartoons from the list given to her. Usually when I get up the next morning there will be a handful of new cartoons in the dropbox folder. It's that simple. I send her payments every 2 weeks using PayPal.

Another great way to bridge the gap when you need to get a project done is to outsource individual projects on a pay-as-you-go basis. It's great if you only want to get a handful of websites designed every year to pay for website instead of hiring a full-time designer and trying to keep them busy. In many cases I hire people this way because I prefer not to make commitments unless I see it lasting a long time. For me the people who fall into this category are programmers, copywriters (although as I write this I am interviewing full-time copywriters), logo designers, template designers, ghost writers, and sometimes image editors.

You can hire people like this on websites like odesk.com and vworker.com. It's great because you can describe your job in detail and then have your choice of bidders. Always look for people with good reputation ratings over low-priced people. I can often get an entire software application written for a few hundred dollars. Again this is the kind of labor that can be outsourced to an emerging economy like India, the Philippines etc.

A great place to get really small jobs done is fiverr.com. This is a place where $5 will buy you anything from basic professional voice over work, artwork, video work, design work, writing and more. Don't expect masterpieces here but if you need something quick and dirty it's a fantastic place. At $5 per video, it doesn't take much to get creative and start thinking about all the kinds of things you might want to shoot that could generate traffic for you.

I once used a $5 video provider to create YouTube video responses to popular videos for me. $5 spent on a good video would generate thousands of clicks per month from the response. It doesn't take much to get content like this to add up. You just have to plan ahead.

The goal of course is to replace as many of the activities you don't want on your plate as possible. I still work a lot because I want to and I enjoy what I do. I just make sure that if I find I'm doing something that I don't enjoy I pass it off to someone else to take over for me. Having the right team in place made it possible for me to write this book. If I was spending all my time answering customer service questions, figuring out how to write software and replying to e-mail I would never have the time available to write my 1st book. But here it is :-)

# NOT CARING WHAT PEOPLE THINK

# Chapter 19: Not Caring What People Think

I like to speak at events. Mainly because of my need to be the center of attention. I used to go to events and watch other speakers and grumble to myself 'I can do a better job than this asshole'. So rather than continue grumbling, I started pitching conference organizers.

One of my very first talks was about search engine optimization to a group of WordPress bloggers in Toronto.

I hadn't figured out yet how important it was to talk about my past. In fact I was so worried that people would boo me off of stage, I avoided mentioning my past in the porn industry.

The night before the event I went to a reception for the speakers. There I spoke to one of the event organizers and he began to probe me about my experience with search engine optimization. Eventually I came clean admitting that I had been in the porn business.

When the organizer introduced me the next day he told the story of our chat the night before. I was mortified. The secret was out, all these people were going to judge me because I was a dirty pornographer.

Much to my surprise the talk went well, but I never once mentioned porn in my talk.

A few months later I was approached by someone who claimed to be working with Jack Canfield you know the Chicken Soup guy.

They told me that Jack wanted to work with me, but they were concerned about my history in the adult business. They even went to the trouble of having lawyers investigate me. I was then told that if I wanted to work with Jack I needed to make sure some of my past was erased.

Before taking on the difficult task of trying to erase my past on the Internet, I met with my friend Scott Stratten.

Scott was already a successful speaker, and his book Unmarketing was about to be published (now a bestseller WAY TO GO MAN!). Scott was where I wanted to be in a couple of years. So I offered to pay him for an hour of his time. He accepted and we met at a coffee shop in Oakville, Ontario.

I told Scott point-blank why I was there. I had a tough decision to make, embrace my past in the porn industry or completely erase it. He made his opinion very clear.

Scott told me that the fact that I was number one for the keyword porn on Google and had tons of great stories about my time in the industry was something that I would be a fool to ignore. Everyone in mainstream knows that the people in adult lead the pack when it comes to online marketing. Trying to bury this would be one of the biggest mistakes I could make.

In hindsight of course he was right. I was smart enough to listen to someone who I paid to coach me rather than let the advice fall on deaf ears. So I immediately started pitching talks to conference organizers that involved me talking about my past in porn.

Needless to say, there won't be any Chicken Soup for the Pornographer's Soul books coming out anytime soon. I learned I have to be willing to let the wrong opportunities go.

Scott later introduced me to Yanik Silver who would later give me one of my first big talks at his Underground Seminar in DC titled: A+ Lessons From an X Rated Industry. The talk went VERY well and I have been getting more and more requests to speak at events. Of course my talk won't work for every audience. I get that, and embrace the audiences that do resonate with my subject matter and style.

Last year a friend of mine asked me to speak to a career class at the local high school. My response to her was simple.

Unless I can talk about my history in the porn business, I will have to decline. You see, I wasn't prepared to sugarcoat my talks. I tried that in the beginning and I hated myself for it.

After some back-and-forth with the teacher, my friend replied and said it's all good.

Fast forward to career day. I didn't realize that I would be sharing the limelight with a multilevel marketer, insurance agent and a police officer. But that's exactly what I had to do.

The insurance agent went first. She painted a picture for the class by telling a story of a man with a mortgage and family who gets into an accident. Clearly this was the wrong audience for her sales pitch, and I don't think any of them were going to go home and convince their parents to buy life insurance. She then proceeded to tell them how she is "passionate about insurance". She must've taken one of those seminars that told her to follow her passion, then she decided that her existing career was her passion. I'm not sure anybody could truly be passionate about insurance, but then what do I know?

Next was the multilevel marketer, I couldn't believe that anyone in the career class was considering a life of meeting people at the coffee shop, explaining compensation plans, science, and potential income. She was pretty smart, a former police officer who was obviously one of the few people who had made multilevel marketing work.

Then it was my turn. I'm not sure the class knew what to expect, I told them I was an Internet marketer first. Then I explained that when I got started in the late 1990s there were only three things on the Internet that made money and they all began with P.

Porn.
Poker.
Pills.

I then explained to them that I wasn't very good at poker, and didn't really like taking pills or selling them. That left me with only one P.

At this point the dudes in the back of the class (they were my crowd, I was those dudes in high school) started paying attention.

After talking about my history in the adult business, what I do now etc. it was now time for the police officer to do his talk.

The first thing the cop told the high school students was that he followed me on Twitter and was excited to see me there. Turns out this cop doesn't like his job, and wants to do what I do for a living. I was pretty shocked, not only do I still smell like weed from the joint I smoked that morning, now this cop wants to be me.

His talk was actually really good. He was extremely honest, telling the class that it's not easy to be a police officer, talked about the high rate of divorce etc.

When it was all over the teacher asked us if we would break out into different rooms with various students for Q&A. He asked all of the speakers to leave the class while he took a poll of who wanted to go and chat with each speaker. I guess I wasn't surprised that I had the biggest crowd followed by the police officer as a close second. The insurance lady and the multilevel marketer had so few students interested in chatting with them that they had to stick together for their Q&A session.

Talking to high school students is a lot of fun. They ask some of the best questions and are genuinely interested in the answers if you are honest with them. I have to say of all the talks I've done this was the most rewarding.

The point of this story isn't to tell you how much cooler I am than the multilevel marketer, police officer or insurance lady. Although clearly I am way cooler than all three combined ;-) it's to illustrate the point that the less I care about the percentage of people who will dislike me the more I connect with the percentage who do.

Let that sink in for a minute.

When you try to please everybody, you fail miserably. Just take a look at anyone in politics. Nobody likes them because they are so washed down that they don't make an impact. Since I'm not running for public office, I am willing to offend more than 50% of any audience.

I remember watching the movie Private Parts about Howard Stern. One of the things that stuck out for me was that the people who loved him were listening every day because they loved him, but the people who hated him were listening every day because they couldn't help themselves. They just wanted to hear what he was going to say next.

I learned that as long as people are talking about you, you are making an impact. I have seen countless message board threads and discussions talking about me in a negative light because I swear, smoke pot, talk about the porn biz etc. I've also seen countless discussions talking about me in a positive light for all the same things and the content that I deliver.

On the Internet when we are making sales, it's usually very good if you can sell 5 - 10% of the people who visit your website.

It's important to point out that you get to choose who those people are. If you aren't 100% genuine, you will have a hard time selling even that small sliver. However if you are yourself, I'm talking about the person you are when you're out with your friends. People who are just like you and your friends will gravitate to you and your products. The more you let go of inhibitions the better you will do in this department.

It doesn't happen overnight. We all want everyone to like us, it's human nature. I've actually taught myself to allow people to hate me and to embrace it when they do. This isn't easy. But the sooner you get this lesson the better off you will be. In fact I would say make it your mission to piss some people off. If you do this effectively, you will create just as many rabid fans as you do haters.

I swear in my e-mails, write blog posts about vaginal cream, take bong hits during video webinars and talk about things the way I do when I'm with my friends or at home with my wife. All of these things have helped me to connect to an audience of people who are just like me. When I travel to events the people who approach me are people who I would like to be friends with. That's an important distinction. When you try to please everyone, the types of people who gravitate to you are often nothing like you at all. But when you are willing to talk about things that others won't, you connect with people on a whole new level.

Everybody I know who is good at personal branding has figured this out along the way. I'm only going to say this one more time. You really do get to choose the people you connect with. Choose them wisely.

I'll tell you another story about why it's so important to be yourself.

I started an advertising company in 2005 called P2P Ads. I had figured out how to monetize peer-to-peer file sharing networks like LimeWire and BitTorrent.

It didn't take me long to get bored, so I sold my share in the company to move on to shinier things. However the company was struggling without me so they called me back to consult with them. Which I did for several months.

Their new CEO who had become a good friend of mine had been making lots of inroads with record companies that might be interested in working with us. When I sold the business we strictly worked in the porn industry, the new CEO was desperately trying to bridge the gap into mainstream.

He landed us a meeting with Sony BMG. This was a very important milestone for the company. I understood the gravity and offered to tag along for the meeting.

When my CEO called me about the meeting time he told me that I needed to dress better than usual for the meeting. I am not someone who likes to get dressed up. I hate wearing pleated dress pants, tucking in my shirt with a collar or otherwise trying to fit in with a bunch of suits.

Going against my better judgment I put on these goofy clothes because it was important to me that the meeting went well.

Upon arriving at the Sony BMG offices I quickly realized both of us were overdressed. It felt pathetic. Here we are in this cool office complete with indoor basketball nets, everyone's wearing jeans but me and my CEO. One of the staff at the office even made a comment about how they are much more casual.

No deal was made during that or any other meeting. Of course the clothing we wore had nothing to do with it but I could definitely not be myself wearing pleated dress pants with my shirt tucked in. So I learned a valuable lesson.

The last time I was asked to dress "business casual" was at a private event for entrepreneurs and business students to go see a man named Brett Wilson speak. Chances are if you aren't Canadian you probably don't know who Brett Wilson is. He is a Canadian entrepreneur who had been on a show called Dragons Den. Which is similar to a show in the United Kingdom with the same name and a show in the United States called Shark Tank.

I was invited to bring one guest and so I asked my dad to come along. An e-mail went out the day of the event telling everyone that business attire was going to be enforced. I thought to myself fuck that I'm a VIP, I can wear whatever I want.

When we got there everyone was wearing a suit, the entrepreneurs, the business students everyone but me. I was the only guy wearing a nice pair of jeans with a decent shirt. That was at least until Brett Wilson came out. He and I were wearing a very similar outfit. Immediately I realized that my choice of attire was awesome.

Just at the moment when I started caring about what others were thinking, I was validated for not caring once again.

Be yourself 100% of the time. And never apologize for that. Ever.

# PRODUCTIVITY

# Chapter 20: Productivity

If you suffer from a lack of focus in business you aren't hungry enough.

I take on some coaching clients in my business. I do this for a couple of reasons. I actually do like to help people and see them succeed. But I also like the easy money that coaching brings me. When you know your content and you know exactly how to help people when they are stuck, coaching is very easy. If you are an awesome poker player you will have an easy time helping novice poker players learn the game.

One of the obstacles that many people face when trying to build a business is a lack of focus. Often coaching clients will ask me to hold them accountable, and stay on top of them to get things done. I explain right away that this is not my role. Olympic athletes don't hire coaches to get them up in the morning to make sure they show up to practice. They hire a coach to help them refine their technique, and push them when they think they are already at their limit. This is how I see my coaching role with clients.

You might have a full-time job. If you're trying to build a business on the side you will always suffer from a productivity problem because your focus is not where it should be and you aren't hungry. If you need to focus on your business might I suggest quitting your day job. For most people this is an extremely scary proposition. However it's the fastest path to becoming a successful entrepreneur.

If you aren't willing to quit your job, my suggestion is to make some financial commitments that are outside of your existing abilities to make payments. Go buy a second house, expensive sports car or something else you can't quite afford today. Nothing motivates us more than having to pay for a bill that's outstanding. I know most people don't give this advice but if you can't focus it's because you're too comfortable. You need to become uncomfortable fast.

If you aren't willing to either quit your job or make a financial commitment that makes you hungry you probably don't have what it takes to be an entrepreneur. Close this book and give it to someone smarter than you, it's likely your business aspirations are just an escape from your life.

Productivity has never been a problem for me because I'm hungry. There have been many times when I've been earning lots of money to the point where the hunger goes away. This is a desirable state for me because it's where I want to be. I don't want to be hungry. But when I am not hungry I also don't want to be productive :-)

People want to be productive because they want to change their lives, they either want to create something that makes them money or get something done. I truly believe that productivity and hunger go hand-in-hand.

Some of the most successful people I know are master delegator's. They outsource everything from having laundry washed and folded, housecleaning etc. Don't hire someone inside your business until you have outsourced as many of your domestic chores as you can.

I have a friend who is a successful perfectionist, a curse for him because he can't let anyone do anything for him. He does all of his own home improvements because he doesn't trust a contractor to do the work. He even cuts his own 10 acre lawn because he doesn't trust a landscaper to do it. Meanwhile he could be spending that time with his friends and family, or working on his business that pays him very well. Don't be that perfectionist.

One of the big mistakes I see new entrepreneurs making is trying to outsource everything. Often I would hear people say I just read The Four Hour Work Week and I want to hire a bunch of outsourcers so I can start my business. Outsourcing is something you do when you are busy, not when you are starting your business.

I'm not saying that you should take on every task yourself. Quite the opposite. If you need a web designer, don't learn how to design a website. Go to 99designs.com. However, people get caught up in the idea of outsourcing to the point where they think they can hire someone in a Third World country to create their products for them.

Best-selling authors don't outsource their books. My wife Claire has a vegan cookbook that sells well on the Internet. Why does it sell well? Because she understood her audience and created a product based on her own experience. She didn't say to herself "I should find someone to create this cookbook for me". There is a big difference.

Instead she outsources her customer support, marketing (to me) and writing for her vegan recipe blog to professional writers. You have to discover what you are good at and focus your time there. Outsource the 80% of your work which doesn't contribute to the bottom line. The more I focus on the work I am best at (preparing presentations, product creation, brainstorming ideas etc.) the more money I make.

The key is figuring out your 80% and finding awesome people to execute for you. I am VERY lucky to have a talented team. It takes work to get people there but you can do it. I usually only hire A-players who are local. I have some offshore staff but only for extremely non-critical tasks.

Okay, so I've talked about the high-level philosophies I have about productivity. But of course there is a technical side to this as well. Here is a short list of my productivity tips.

**1. Separate your office.**
Use a door, separate building or just make your friends and family aware that you need to be left alone when working. If you have kids this goes double for you. Family must respect workspace. Also remember that people may start thinking because you work from home you are always free for coffee or whatever. Be ruthless with your time. I know part of this is being able to enjoy your freedom, but if you were planning to work today then work. Being your own boss means sometimes being bossy with yourself.

**2. Avoid email at all costs.**
This won't be easy for most of you. But I am what I like to call email bankrupt. Everyone knows you can't email me. I HATE email because it's the biggest productivity killer I know of. Especially when it's checking your inbox for new items every 15 mins. No wonder we all have A.D.D. My assistant, Megan handles all my email exchanges. Not as me but as my assistant.

One client complained that it would be easier to reach god than me, I told him that Megan was doing her job then, and well.

## 3. If you must work with clients make them pay for their first meeting.

Nothing weeds out the people who want to waste your time than charging for a first meeting. In my first meetings with companies I leave them with so much knowledge and ideas that I need to charge for the meeting. Too often they go do it all on their own then call again when they are stuck. The people who know your value will gladly pay. You are sitting down to talk about THEIR business. It's their hour. Make them pay. Every time.

## 4. Try to work in 90 minute chunks

My friend Evan Carmichael taught me this in one of our mastermind meetings. After about 90 mins you start to lose focus, so take a 15-30 minute break, have a snack and recharge. It's not easy and seems counterintuitive but it makes a huge difference how focused you get in those 90 minute bursts.

## 5. Avoid social networking

During the work day, try to avoid Facebook, Twitter etc. If you must use these tools schedule the time. It's amazing how much changes on Facebook when you don't visit every 5 mins.

## 6. Exercise regularly

Nothing beats feeling strong and physically fit. Donny Deutsch said in his book 'Often Wrong, Never in Doubt' that it makes negotiating business deals much easier when you know you can kick the guys ass on the other side of the table. I can't agree more. My mind works better when my body is fit. I am not the best at maintaining this all the time but I am constantly improving.

### 7. Meditate
Meditation is a way to give yourself some daily stillness. It's a ritual for calming the mind. You won't go to hell for meditating, but you will feel much more balanced and calm throughout even the hardest days.

### 8. Mono-task don't multitask
Multitasking was supposed to make us all more productive. Instead it made us into retards with the attention span of a carrot stick. There are a few exceptions. I like to take calls while driving because I can drive and carry on a conversation. But I won't take a phone call while at my computer because you can't do it without losing focus on the call. Try to avoid running 8 software apps and trying to dabble in each one. Nothing gets done well. I used to be so guilty of this. At one stage I had 7 screens on my desk. I am down to 4. Someone please do an intervention. I only need 3 ;)

### 9. Ask your people "what would you do if this was your business?"
Sometimes when an employee asks you to make a decision, ask them what they would do. Often they have insights you don't or a better handle on the situation but are coming for advice out of habit. It teaches them and you that they are capable of making judgement calls without you. An important step in minimizing your own role in day to day functions.

### 10. Never learn how to do something just so you can do it yourself (unless you truly have interest in the topic).

I am learning copywriting right now. It takes a long time to get good at it but I am truly interested in the psychology of selling people with words on a page or video. But while I learn I still hire professional copy writers to help with sales copy because I make 2x more revenue with professional copy than my own. Some things are NOT worth doing yourself to save a few bucks.

## 11. Buy traffic

If you are creating products and waiting for Google to feed you free traffic you failed internet marketing. You don't have a business if you can't figure out how to spend $1 and make $1.50. Why invest countless hours "link building" or writing articles to promote a product that won't sell? Put your offer to the test with paid traffic, optimize your process until it profits or proves itself unworthy.

## 12. Use dictation software

You might be surprised to know that over 90% of this book was dictated. I use a software app called Dragon dictation. It's simple. I only type if it's a short message. Everything else is dictated and I can put out more words per minute than any professional secretary in the history of the world. I never paid enough attention in typing class and being a large guy I have extremely large fingers (that's RIGHT ladies) so I hate typing and I can't do it very fast.

## 13. Learn to wake up naturally

Something occurred to me recently. I actually had to do some math. I have woken up over 5000 times without an alarm clock. When I had a job, I woke up to an alarm. Most mornings it startled me out of bed and started my day off in the worst possible way. With a nagging alarm sound telling me it's time to go to my shitty job. When I became a full-time entrepreneur I immediately started sleeping in. But over time something happened that I thought was very interesting. When I was in my early 20s I could sleep till noon any time I was given the option. Today I couldn't do that if you paid me. Naturally I get up between 7 and 8 AM every morning. Even when I go to Las Vegas and party until 4 AM, my body naturally wakes me up around 8 o'clock the next morning. It's not always a good thing but I believe by letting my body wake me up at a natural time over 5000 times since becoming a full-time entrepreneur has had an extremely positive effect on my health, and my productivity.

**14. Buy a Macintosh computer**
Okay, call me a Mac fan boy I can take it. It really has nothing to do with that for me. I don't want the cool thing as much as I want the functional thing. In the beginning my office used PCs. We had entire days where employees couldn't work while we cleaned those PCs of spyware, viruses etc. Office productivity was at 0% on those days. That cost me more than any savings realized by cheaping out on PCs. By using Macintosh computers, not only are myself and my staff more productive, the work we do is way better. Macs are made for creative people. Most of the built-in software allows you to do everything you need to make intangible products. You can make your own music, write an e-book, edit a movie or create a presentation that comes out looking extremely slick. And it's all done with cheap software and way more easily than you can imagine.

**15. Use mind mapping software**
It took me a while to come around. I didn't like the idea of spending too much time planning, but I've discovered mind

maps are extremely intuitive way to get everything from inside your head into a document. It's actually a very liberating feeling. When I have an idea buzzing around in my head I often can't focus on watching a movie or listening to my wife talk. If I spend some time mapping it out into a simple mind map, a weight is lifted and I get instant clarity. It also lets me look at my idea and all of its pieces at a glance. There are plenty of free mind mapping tools out there. I personally like my iPad version of ithoughts HD.

**16. Go paperless**
Okay I know we have been promised a paperless office since the late 1980's but it's actually possible today. We use a Fujitsu ScanSnap document scanner to dump double sided documents to EverNote. Everything becomes searchable and easy to retrieve from multiple locations and it's backed up in the cloud.

I can even take pictures with my EverNote iphone app and it will recognize the text in every photo.

The last thing I will mention about productivity has more to do with internal attitude.

It's important to go into every project with a clear vision of success. There is no room for self doubt when creating things from scratch. You need to see a positive outcome and convince the people who work with you of that vision. You and the people you work with need to create a culture of decisiveness. It's okay to play devil's advocate once in a while when important decisions are being made so that you consider all of your options. But once you've made a decision it's important to execute on that decision without any further doubt. That's what good leaders do. Your team will quickly lose faith in you if you are constantly revisiting old decisions and struggling with them. In my experience people who can make quick decisions and then make decisions on top of those decisions are always more successful than people who take their time or revisit old choices with doubt.

# PERSONAL BRANDING

# Chapter 21: Personal Branding

*Gentlemen, (I am being some what respectful)*
*I was on your webinar this evening and you had no regard, respect or concern for your audience. When you were warned by your listeners that they did not want to hear your filthy mouths, your cavalier response was appalling! It quickly told me what kind of professionals you were, therefore I promptly ended my side of the webinar and quickly decided there was nothing good I could learn from you and immediately chose right away not to buy any of your products! I SHUT DOWN!*

*Perhaps you should both change careers and go to work in a filthy mouthed comedy club where you will be widely accepted. I'm sure a pro like Dave Lakhani would never insult his audience like you did this evening. Perhaps you need a refresher course in sales and dealing with the public. My wife once told me, people that use foul language, had nothing more intelligent to say! I hope you clean up your act and change your attitude or your online webinar's will be empty when word gets around!*

*Sincerely,*
*name removed*
*Northern Virginia*
*PS. Please remove me from any further lists or communications! I wish you the best in your filthy mouthed comedy club acts?*

Don't be afraid to let people hate you…

Most people would be mortified to receive an e-mail like the one above. I on the other hand was ecstatic. You see, this gentleman either missed the opening of the webinar or just really wanted to stick around because we gave fair warning about the foul language in advance. I always do. Most of my webinars start with "be forewarned, I like to use foul language and tell dirty jokes. If you have your speakers on, or your kids will overhear, I suggest getting some headphones or tuning out this webinar."

This one lesson is by far the most important one I have learned since I began my branding journey.

It seems counterintuitive, but I lead with this point for a reason. It's not your goal to make people hate you. If it was, it would be pretty easy to just do some really terrible things like killing puppies on the Internet. Instantly everyone would hate you. You don't want everyone to hate you, but it's okay if half of the people do.

In my case I have a fair number of people who dislike me. Possibly because of my history in the adult entertainment business. Or maybe it's because I'm not afraid to talk about drugs, make sick jokes and swear. In fact I hosted a webinar the other night, and watched the chat. A good number of people were absolutely outraged at my language. I warned them before I even started that I was going to be swearing. The funny thing is, they couldn't leave. Even though they can't stand me, they can't bring themselves to turn it off.

The guy above even made a comment about how there are plenty of good comedians out there who don't need to use foul language. I checked on Netflix, I couldn't find any.

When you try to blend in you wind up like a politician. Nobody likes or listens to your mediocre babble.

Okay so hopefully you get my point about being yourself. The closer your brand image is to your true self the easier life will be for you. Of course you can't build your brand overnight. But you can start off on the right foot. Here are a few things to make sure you do right from the start.

Hire a professional photographer. For you to establish a brand online, you need to have a professional photographer take some good memorable photos of you. I'm not talking about Sears portrait studio styles here. Don't even think about going to Walmart to get your photo taken. You need someone who can help you bring out your personality in your photographs. I do a few interesting things when I get my picture taken. As I think about how to put this into words I realize how narcissistic this will make me sound but, oh well, fuck it.

Make sure to get some photos of you where the photographer is physically below you. The camera should be pointed up at you while you are seated in a comfortable position looking down slightly at the lens. Images like this create a perspective where you are in the power position. My friends have joked with me to the point of putting crowns on my head in Photoshop and reposting the pictures. Everyone laughed including me. I get how ridiculous it is but it works. I'm not saying you should look down at people in every photo. Most recently I have been using pictures of myself speaking from stage. The photographer is always below me when I speak from stage. Pictures of you speaking from stage scream authority. It's true what they say about a picture being worth 1000 words.

The pictures you take will be used to create websites, social profiles, webinars etc. so make sure they are awesome. Also make sure to include some fun shots of you that will be memorable. At all costs, avoid wearing something out of character. And try to avoid typical poses.

Register your name as a domain. If you haven't already done this it might be hard to get yourname.com but there are plenty of other extensions like .me that will do just fine. Use a hosting company that allows WordPress websites and install a video friendly theme.

Set up social profiles. Don't think of this as a spray and pray approach. Many people will go and sign up at 100 different social bookmark and networking websites, only to complain later that there aren't enough hours in the day to maintain all of them. DUH. Instead, focus on the few where you think you can be the most effective. For me those are Facebook, Twitter, YouTube and Flickr. I do have profiles on other websites such as LinkedIn however I don't spend much time maintaining those profiles.

I use Facebook because all my friends are there. It's a great place for me to post pictures, links to promotions etc. I'm often surprised at how many real world friends purchase and consume my products. Think of It this way, Facebook is the largest social network in the English-speaking world. Everyone should maintain a profile there.

Setting up a Facebook profile doesn't mean going out and adding random people you don't know as friends. Stick to the people you know in the real world. Having a few thousand

Facebook friends isn't all that great. Especially when you went out hunting for all of them. I started my Facebook profile by adding only people who I had met in the real world. Eventually friends of friends would start adding me etc. I accept most friend requests.

I use Twitter mainly because Internet marketers spend a lot of time on Twitter. For most people it's not really necessary. Personally I'm finding it to be less relevant. Having said that, at the time of writing this book I have over 30,000 followers. So of course I'm going to maintain a profile because the audience there is quite large. One of the cool things about Twitter is that people who like you tend to repeat, a.k.a. retweet what you say, links etc.

I personally have an account on Flickr.com because I like to take pictures. I am a bit of an amateur photographer. Flickr is kind of like YouTube but for photographs. It's not as much a social network as it is a content network. My photos collectively have millions of views.

I use YouTube because I'm a big believer in creating video if you want to propel your personal brand. Shooting video where you talk to the camera is the easiest and fastest way to get people's attention. It's so important because the written word lacks tonality. When you speak to your audience they can feel your emotion, sense your sincerity and see your facial expressions.

The most important factor contributing to my personal brand and my success is video. Keep in mind, my very first videos were absolutely terrible. In fact they sucked. Watching them now is painful. Your first videos are going to suck too. I promise you that. Just don't be afraid to let them suck. If you struggle for perfection, you will never publish anything. My guess is this book has typos. Fuck it.

I literally have hundreds of videos floating around the Internet. In fact at any given minute someone is likely watching one of my videos or listening to my voice.

Video made it possible for me to get my first speaking gigs. It also makes me instantly recognizable at events. But probably the coolest thing, is that it creates bonds with people all over the world. I can charge someone $20,000 for coaching who has never met me before because they have seen almost all of my content and it resonated with them. People often say to me "I feel like I already know you". To me this is a huge compliment.

Some of my most popular videos have been somewhat unexpected. I'll give you a few examples.

**Going behind the scenes.**
We had been shooting these videos on a white background using some good camera equipment, cheap lighting, a photographer's backdrop etc. and I kept getting messages from people asking how we did it. So I decided to shoot a video explaining how we shoot videos. I actually didn't think many people were going to be interested but I did it anyway because it was easy. It started off with me talking on my white backdrop. Then I flashed a few people's questions from Twitter. My wife Claire was shooting the video and a couple of minutes in she zoomed out the camera to show me in my kitchen sitting at my breakfast bar.

Everything behind the scenes was instantly revealed. I then picked up a flip cam and pointed it towards the camera so everyone could see what I was seeing. This video has been seen thousands of times and continues to get fantastic comments and feedback.

**Sharing the news.**
One day while taking a shit I was reading WIRED magazine. In this particular issue there was an interview with Google engineers. They answered some interesting questions about changes to their algorithm. Because I am into search engine optimization, I fired up my flip camera and started talking about the article and what I learned from it. This video was picked up by several influential SEO bloggers which helped to raise my profile among SEO people.

**Talking about mistakes.**
One of the toughest things that happened to me in this business was getting a website slapped by Google. I ranked at the top for the single word porn. That is until we got penalized for buying and selling links. This website was getting 250,000 visitors a day. Losing that position was very tough on my ego and bank account. So shooting a video to talk about it was not easy. In fact I waited until a full year later because interestingly enough on the 366th day, they placed my website right back at the top. So I shot a video talking about it. What I wasn't prepared for was the number of views and the number of comments in general. I got tons of feedback from people who had been in a similar situation.

Additionally I got tons of comments from people making fun of the way I pronounce "penalize". I say pee-na-ly-zze. That's right.

Sharing your losses can help you to connect with people often better than sharing your successes. We can all sympathize with critical mistakes.

Here are some of the pictures I currently use to brand myself online.

Me looking down at camera ;)

Claire, Me, Megan 2009

Mercedes SLS AMG 2011

Audi R8 2011

Playboy Mansion 2007

**YOU ARE NOT SCALABLE**
**YOUR CONTENT IS**

# Chapter 22: You Are Not Scalable, Your Content Is

I originally learned this lesson from my friend Rajesh Setty. So props to you my friend :-)

The principle behind this is simple. Imagine you have a web design company, and you're just starting out. Someone tells you that you should be cold calling businesses.

If in an 8 hour day you are able to make 100 cold calls, you might be lucky to get 2 or 3 prospects each day.

To someone just starting out, 2 to 3 new prospects each day hoping that at least one becomes a customer might sound pretty good. But then you have to stop making cold calls to service your customers, and then the cycle begins of feast and famine. You're not really a business owner, you are a slave to your profession.

If instead of making 100 cold calls, you shot 4 extremely effective videos, maybe giving advice to potential clients about how to choose a good web designer, questions to ask or perhaps providing a PDF checklist for small business websites. Those 4 videos, could be seen by thousands of people over the next few months.

Don't spin your wheels trying to generate business. Avoid your local Chamber of Commerce networking meetings, the people who go to those meetings are all in the same boat as you, they are trying to sell. It's like going to a singles bar packed with straight men who have boners. Nobody's getting laid.

Cold calling and networking are not scaleable activities. You can only hustle for so many hours each day. Unless you love to hustle.

Focus your time on creating and distributing great content. Buy advertising to feed to your content, offers, list building opportunities etc.

This also applies to things like customer support. As you are building your business, it might seem like extra work to film a tutorial video instead of just firing off an e-mail response to a customer. But think about it this way, every time a customer asks you a question, it's likely the same question will come up again and again. Wouldn't it be smarter to have a video tutorial that answers the question? You could post it in your knowledge base, support pages or just have canned responses by e-mail linking to the videos.

The difference between working harder and working smarter is often a question of scale. So many of my customers have trouble with the basics, so I created an entire training website called Newbie Camp. Any time a coaching client asks me a basic question about how to set up their autoresponder or something to do with WordPress etc. I send them to Newbie Camp. Explaining that they pay me far too much money to sit there with them live helping them with basics. It saves me time and headaches and saves them money. Everyone wins.

It takes time to create good content, but it's worth the effort. I create content on a regular basis and blast it out to thousands of people. If I create a single piece of content that's 5 minutes long, and 1000 people watch it, I will have saved 83 hours of my time. Simply by scaling my content.

# TRAIN PEOPLE TO DEAL WITH YOU

# Chapter 23: Train People To Deal With You

It doesn't matter who you are working with. Partners, clients, affiliates, customers, investors etc.

You need to train people in how to deal with you. Often in personal development and sales training books they tell you to match the behavior of the person you are working with in order to get their attention and respect. In my experience everyone reacts differently to every situation. You can't match everyone's behavior all the time, and especially when they are acting ridiculously.

That means, setting the tone for how you do things immediately.

Everyone who works with me knows that I don't read e-mail. I have literally decided it's not for me because it's such a waste of time. My assistant reads my e-mail and tells me what I need to know and responds accordingly. I have trained them this way by not engaging in e-mail at all. Some people don't like it but I set their expectations immediately. I always tell people "I don't do e-mail". Sometimes they laugh but when they realize I'm not joking they adapt. There are plenty of other ways to get a hold of me if you have access.

I once had a client who wanted me to work with him. My minimum at the time was $7000. He came to visit me and gave me a 50% deposit. He left with 100% of his product.

About a month later, I was in the middle of running a seminar in Toronto. It was the same week as my birthday. My wife had purchased a new iPhone for me and it was to be a surprise. The problem was that my voicemail wasn't working on the old phone. But because I was running a seminar I couldn't be bothered to worry about voicemail. So I just ignored it for 3 days. This is a VERY common practice for me.

On the last day of my seminar I got a very frantic text message from my client. Now keep in mind this guy already had his product in hand. He needed my help with something but I was not available.

I responded by text to let him know I was at my seminar and I wouldn't be able to reach him for a few more days. Once I got home I was able to listen to my voice mail messages. This guy went from happy to borderline insane in a matter of 48 hours. I was not on call for this gentleman and for all he knew I was on vacation.

I responded by e-mailing him the following week. My response was simple. I would not tolerate this behavior any longer and the next time I hear one angry voicemail from you, we will block all communication going forward. I was willing to fire this customer over his anger management problem.

Once he realized how serious I was, he apologized for his behavior and explained he was under several other external pressures. Usually when someone has an emergency, it's their emergency not yours. Don't let them make it your emergency. The first time you do this you will set a dangerous precedent. People will learn that they can come to you in the last minute and make you drop everything because they yell and scream.

Or simply ask you to. It doesn't matter what the behavior is like, if you have other projects to do, don't drop everything. Unless you charge a whole lot extra to do so.

I can't tell you how many times I have fired clients. I usually give them a warning and then they're gone. It may seem harsh but you didn't start a business to take shit from other people. The first time you let them dump it on you you are showing them you are shit bucket, and training them to dump on you. If you resist, you are training them to treat you with respect. There is nothing more important than getting respect. Life is so much easier when the people you work with observe those basics.

I'll give you one more story about this. One of our employees had made friends with a local country singer who was trying to make a name for herself. Her website was terrible and he asked us several times if we could work with her at a discount to help her with her career. Reluctantly my partner Justin and I met with her and her "manager". This girl hadn't gone very far beyond singing at a few county fairs.

When she came into our office it was clear she thought she was way more important than we did. She acted as if she was doing us a favor because we were going to ride the success bus with her all the way to Nashville. She immediately tried to put us on trial as if she was paying thousands and thousands of dollars for our services. She asked questions like why should I work with you etc.

By the end of the meeting, it was clear to us that she would be a problem client at any price level. Never-mind working with her at cost. So the next day her manager called me. He had good news. They had decided to give us a shot and work with us. He was not going to like my response.

Me: "We have actually decided not to work with you going forward, I wish you both the best of luck"

Manager: "excuse me?"

Me: "did you misunderstand? We won't be working with you."

Manager: "Are you crazy? Why would you have wasted our time like that?"

Me: "it's clear to me that your client has extremely high expectations for someone with no money. We were willing to do our best to help a local artist, however even if she was paying full price this wouldn't be a fit."

Manager: "you will regret this"

I don't even remember the country singer's name. The only thing I regret is the hour I spent listening to her talk out of her ass in my office.

Sometimes you have to train people to not deal with you at all. That's cool too :-)

Just remember rules are MUCH easier to set in advance. People respect you more when you create social contracts and stick to them.

# DEALING WITH ASSHOLES

# Chapter 24: Dealing With Assholes

One of the unfortunate side effects of running an Internet business is the number of assholes you have to deal with.

Mainly because people don't have to show their face to you ever on the Internet, they can bring out their true hateful self. Of course not everyone you deal with on the Internet will be an asshole. But you will have to deal with them.

Often times the medium is more important than anything else. Dealing with an asshole on Twitter is very different to dealing with one on a message board. I spend a lot of time on a message board known as the warrior forum. They call it that because it's where you do battle with assholes.

There are number of strategies that I have found to work. Often the best one is to ignore. In most cases these people move on to new targets. In the case where I'm trying to sell something on a message board, I can't ignore negative comments about my products.

Most of the time it's just someone who's trying to outsmart me. They think by contradicting something I say they can feel better about themselves. I often reply with something smarter than they can comprehend and then they disappear.

The worst kind of asshole, is the one who hates you. Remember me telling you to let people hate you? ;-) Well there will be some aftermath.

These people, often after a 32 hour stint at World of Warcraft show up in your sales threads or social comment streams dropping all kinds of hate. They are often challenging to deal with because their only goal is to make things difficult for you.

The great thing about the Internet is people have a profile history. Often the easiest way to deal with someone is to look at the other things they've done online. In the case of a message board you can easily look at the other posts from that person. Chances are if they are being an asshole to you, that will be the general tone of their other posts. This immediately makes them a target.

I most often reply to people like this by saying: "Looking at your other posts in this forum, I can see the tone is mostly negative. You need to turn your frown upside down mister."

I recently did a post on Facebook about how I like to swear and make dirty jokes in my webinars. I got tons of comments from people who thought it was great that I was uncensored. And then one angry person saying that it was childish to swear and that he grew out of that. He then went on in several instances complaining about how people who swear display a lack of intelligence.

Rather than immediately arguing with him, I looked at his Facebook profile. It was clear to me why he was so upset. His status updates were littered with Bible quotes.

My response to him changed from argument to commentary. I simply replied by saying: "judging by the Bible quotes on your Facebook wall you are not in my demographic"

This will often throw your asshole into a rage. When they self-destruct, you can ask for their post to be removed. Often times they will get themselves banned. The point is not to anger the asshole, but instead to show everyone else their true colors. Negative responses in threads where you're trying to sell something as in the warrior forum, can hurt your sales. If dealt with properly however, they can not only help your sales, they can help your personal brand.

For the most part I don't personally deal with the majority of the assholes I do business with. That job falls on my assistant and support staff. I am so thankful for them.

The only assholes I have to deal with are the public ones. Don't be afraid to stand up for yourself and do battle, but do it wisely. Personal attacks won't win you anything, but pushing buttons and pointing out flaws in a smart and witty way will always make you look good.

Other kinds of assholes you will have to deal with online include serial refunders, people who file payment disputes and chargebacks, people who write negative reviews about you on their blog and people on your list who complain that you sell too much. For the most part all of these people can be ignored. I blacklist people who refund my products or file chargebacks. I ignore most negative reviews about my products, although if something is incorrect I will leave a comment on the blog. Bloggers who delete my comments show their true colors.

As for people who complain about you selling too much, tell them to fuck off. Don't ever let someone complaining change your marketing strategy. My attitude is pretty simple, buy something or get the fuck off my list.

# WATCH OUT FOR SOCIAL MEDIA HIPPIES

# Chapter 25: Watch Out For Social Media Hippies

There's a group of people on the Internet, I call them social media hippies. They believe everything should be free, and that you should give everything away in order to create value.

On the surface the principle is great. We all need to give away content in order to scale our brand awareness, but you need to draw the line.

I was asked to speak at a WordPress developers conference known as Word Camp in Detroit. I was delivering the keynote address which was called Your Business Starts With WordPress.

The funny thing was, there was a group of bloggers who were absolutely disgusted that someone was there talking about business. This group somehow saw the world as operating without money and without commerce. They believed I was somehow going against their culture. What they don't understand is that business pays the bills that allow them to be bloggers.

There are lots of ways for people to be homeless bloggers. Literally. Homeless people with blogs. You don't have to have a dime to be a blogger. You can walk into an Apple store every day, log onto the Internet with one of their computers and write a blog entry. It's been done.

Just remember, if you want to make money, you can't listen to homeless people.

Many times these people are not serious about what they do at all. Often they have a spouse or parent supporting them which means I can't relate. Don't let their opinions steer you away from your goal of total freedom.

There are no shortage of social media hippies with best-selling books, huge Twitter followings and a great stage presence. Often these people will convince you that you need to cater to the homeless hippies in order to succeed. This is simply not the case. Never be afraid to ask for money.

Any time someone gives you shit when you ask for money, don't be afraid to tell them to fuck off. Those people are broke. They are complaining about their own state of affairs, not the fact that you are charging. Never forget this.

# ANALYSIS PARALYSIS

# Chapter 24: Analysis Paralysis

One of the biggest mistakes I see people making who want to get started with a new business, is over analyzing every detail.

For some reason the Internet marketing world suffers from this in the worst way. I often wind up coaching people who tell me they have spent years of their life and sometimes 6 figures trying to learn the ins and outs of Internet marketing. And the worst part is they haven't actually created anything.

I've been doing this pretty much since the beginning. One thing I have learned is that I don't need to learn it all. But when I do need to learn something, it's often much cheaper and much faster for me to throw myself into something than it is to buy a book, or take a course. When I wanted to learn Facebook advertising, I started buying ads. I may have spent a few thousand dollars on trial and error, but fast forward to today, I have a keen understanding of what works and what doesn't on Facebook.

Taking someone else's course and learning by their examples would not have given me that level of expertise. So for me it's counterintuitive to try and learn everything before I do anything.

Another big mistake I see people making is over planning. I have a friend who has a ton of spreadsheets on his laptop. Each one projecting sales based on a multitude of variables for his various business ideas. Rather than rolling up his sleeves and getting down to the work of building a business he will project years of growth in revenue on a spreadsheet. The problem with revenue projections and spreadsheets is that they all come down to having to guess at certain numbers. That makes the whole damn thing a joke. If you have all kinds of calculations relying on other numbers that were just guesses, the whole spreadsheet is worthless in my opinion.

It's much better to take 30 to 90 days of real commerce statistics from your business and project future revenue. But that requires doing the work. Most people would rather keep their nose buried in their spreadsheets analyzing business models and projecting revenue.

I'm not saying that there isn't a case for learning new things through guides, courses and books. I do it all the time and I always learn new things whenever I do. However this type of learning requires a lot of free time. If you are in startup mode, this is time you don't have to fool around with. You're much better off getting down to work than you are analyzing and learning.

If you can't get yourself out of this rut, you need to start asking yourself some very hard questions.

Do you really have what it takes to start a business?
Are you afraid of other people's opinions?
Do you lack confidence?
Is all of this analysis a distraction from something else?

The most successful entrepreneurs I know make decisions very quickly often based on their gut feeling. They then make decisions on top of those decisions without blinking. Only a truly confident leader can do this effectively. You need to be a leader if you want to be a successful entrepreneur. Most people who overanalyze things do so because they are used to taking their orders from someone above them. It's a security blanket. If your boss tells you to do it and it doesn't work out, you were just doing what the boss told you. But when you have to make a decision on your own and things don't work out, you have to take responsibility for those decisions.

Some people just don't have what it takes. And that's okay.

# THE GRASS IS NEVER GREENER

# Chapter 26: Grass Is Never Greener

If you are like me you probably have A.D.D.

The mistake I made early on in my business was I would look at other business owners and think they must have it easier than me. Somehow they figured out a way to make it all work while I was still struggling.

Often I would be on to something profitable but constantly looking at other opportunities. Somebody always tells a story about their friend who has it so easy. They only work a small number of hours and make so much money it's disgusting. Whenever we hear the stories, we think about how nice it must be to have it so easy.

Many people will take the sad journey of jumping into a business because of some story.

Here's how the stories get created.

When I first started out on my own, my wife and I bought our house with money we made from a handful of porn sites. One of our family members made a comment to me that I will never forget. It was his first time at my house, and he said to me "it's amazing what a few websites will buy".

In his mind, we had spent a few days building websites, and never worked again. We were just reaping the rewards of those few days of work. Unfortunately I let the comment go. I'm a pretty passive guy and I don't like to engage in arguments. I prefer to let people think they are right than argue with them.

A couple of years later we went to a party at the same family member's house. One of their friends made a comment to my wife and I about how it must be nice to have our lifestyle where we only work a couple of hours a week and make all kinds of money.

At the time, we were actually working very hard on our businesses. Often 50 to 60 hours per week. It was upsetting to hear this, but I realized how these stories get out of hand. By the time the story gets to you, it's a millionaire who presses 3 buttons on his computer every day. Then of course you start thinking about how green the grass must be for that guy.

I've seen this happen over and over again. Especially when I was in the adult business.

I actually made quite a bit of money selling an adult business opportunity to people who have this mentality of greener grass. Being in the adult business generates a lot of attention whether you want it or not.

When I was in the business, it wasn't uncommon for a news story to come out about some rich porn tycoon making money from home. People would see these stories and start asking their friends if they knew anyone in the business. I would often get a different request each week from an old high school friend, friend of a friend or someone I didn't even know asking how I could help them get into the adult business.

You see, a lot of guys think the porn business is glamorous. They like the idea of hanging out with porn stars and models. And they think it's all fun.

The reality is quite different. It's a business riddled with problems and headaches just like every other business.

So if you catch yourself thinking the grass is greener for someone else, thinking that they have none of the problems you have, think again. If you have something that's making you money, focus on it more, not less. It's very easy to jump from one project to the next because each new opportunity looks better. But the real money is made by focusing on projects until they are profitable, and then scaling them.

# DON'T BE AFRAID
## TO ASK FOR MONEY

# Chapter 27: Don't Be Afraid To Ask For Money

When I first began my personal branding journey, I was very open on social media. People would contact me and ask me to meet them for coffee. Stupidly I would say yes, go and sit with them at my local Starbucks, give them free advice and watch them walk away.

At first it didn't bother me because I thought that these people were taking my advice.

One time I met with a guy who wanted to quit his job and provide a better life for his family. He bought the coffee, I asked questions and doled out advice. I only spent an hour with the guy, went home and went on with life and business.

Roughly 6 months later, this guy contacted me again. This time he was desperate. He just got laid off from his job. Desperately asking me what he should do next. Of course by now you know what I asked him…

Me: "did you do all the things I told you to do 6 months ago?"

Him: "no, I never got around to it"

Me: "how about you do the things I told you to do 6 months ago"

Him: "but now I need a quicker fix"

Me: "what's your budget for coaching?"

Him: "well now I am broke, so I can't really afford coaching"

Me: "here's your last bit of free advice, go get another job. Goodbye"

I learned the most valuable lesson that day. People don't take free advice. And successful entrepreneurs don't take free meetings with anyone. Today I charge $997 for a one-hour coffee meeting. I will even buy the coffee :-)

People will often contact my assistant asking me for an initial consultation meeting. They expect this to be free. I never have these meetings without charging for the hour. Remember this, a consultation meeting is where you sit down with a potential client and they talk about their business. The meeting is about them, it's not about you. If they aren't willing to pay for the first hour, they certainly won't be willing to pay for any additional hours. This weeds out people who are broke.

In my experience, the smaller percentage of people who are willing to pay you for your initial meeting are the people you want to work with. If you're going to do any kind of coaching or consulting, you need to establish your worth up front. Don't act like a personal injury attorney. Let them do the free consultations. Let your prospects know your hourly rate upfront. Ask them to pay in advance for their first meeting.

I have built some amazing long-term relationships with clients who have paid for their first meeting. These people are often high functioning entrepreneurs just like me. They understand the value of time. They start their calls on time and finish them on time. They never waste my minutes.

Most entrepreneurs learn this the hard way just like I did. However if I had been smart, I would have been charging for my time even when I wasn't in such demand. I would have weeded out people like the example above. Either he would've paid for the meeting because he had a job at the time and could afford it, or would have tried to find another sucker to spend an hour with.

The psychology behind this is also interesting. People who really want to meet with you will often get upset about you charging a fee, when they realize you don't care, they will often cough up the money.

There is a good strategy for how to deal with this. I always delegate fee and payment discussions to my assistant. When people contact me directly through social media, instant messages, or after a talk, I will often tell them to book an appointment through my assistant Megan and provide her e-mail address.

This passes the buck so to speak. When Megan informs them of their options for payment, they are now dealing with a third-party whose job it is to collect payment in exchange for appointments. I am no longer in communication. I have essentially created a wall. Now they have to deal with my gatekeeper.

If I asked for the money directly, I would deal with much more resistance. When people are passed off to an assistant, they feel more obligated to follow your protocol. We actually provide a few different tiers of pricing. Often pointing people to online training materials, and products I have created. Those options are often much cheaper than working with me one-on-one. The top tier of course is working with me by the hour. But by giving them multiple choices, they don't feel like we have our hands in their pockets. I even offer free advice via Twitter. Although it's very hard for someone to tell you their life story over Twitter, because it only allows 140 characters per message. Which makes giving advice there easy for me.

I guarantee that people will argue with you over this point. Some of those people will be potential clients. It's easy for me because I'm simply in a position to say no. I am so busy and in so much demand that I don't need every client. And I certainly don't need to meet with anyone for free. The sooner you get into this mindset the sooner you will be in high demand.

# CHAMBER OF COMMERCE
# & OTHER ASSOCIATIONS

# Chapter 28: Chamber Of Commerce And Other Associations

When I first started my adult entertainment business, I learned to dislike most organizations.

Because I had an office in a business district I was often visited by salespeople from groups like my local Chamber of Commerce, Better Business Bureau, business improvement associations and more.

Each one of them had an opportunity to take my money because I was naïve enough to think I needed these organizations to help me build my business. Inevitably, I would tell them I was in the pornography business and each one would leave with my check in hand, only to return a few days later saying that the organization didn't actually want me as a member because of what my business did.

Of course I didn't need these groups, as much as they needed my money. But apparently my money was too dirty for them which was just fine for me.

Eventually I made the transition out of the adult business and into a more mainstream focus. Again I took the bait and joined my local Chamber of Commerce thinking that they would help me somehow.

I knew more about Internet marketing than anyone in my town. So after joining my Chamber of Commerce my friend Justin Popovic and I approached them to do a talk for free to small businesses about social media marketing. There was nothing to be sold at the end we just wanted to make a name for ourselves and deliver some value.

We were treated as if we were selling AIDS tainted needles. They weren't interested in social media because it was too early and even though we were members they immediately dismissed us and told us no thanks.

The things we were teaching back then have made us and our clients millions of dollars in returns. It was way ahead of its time, and would have helped a good number of chamber members to increase their bottom line. I say this with complete confidence because I have the benefit of hindsight. The methods we were teaching worked back then and work even better now.

The funny thing is, I didn't renew my membership and a couple of years later one of their organizers contacted me to quote them on doing a social media talk. They couldn't afford me, then and now I am WAY outside their price range.

Just think, if they had been the least bit helpful when I needed them and wanted so badly to deliver value for free, they might have made a friend who was willing to give back. Instead I'm writing a chapter in my book telling everyone who will listen to avoid joining local associations. Take that bitches!

These days the Chamber of Commerce doesn't really offer much. They have golf tournaments, but you can go even if you're not a member. They offer networking breakfasts. Except everyone who goes to those things has something to sell and no budget to buy anything.

A word about the Better Business Bureau. They also wouldn't take my membership when I sold porn. I learned something interesting about that group. Being a member of the Better Business Bureau attracts customers who are high maintenance. People who expect you to be a member are either problem customers or they work for the Better Business Bureau.

If someone is telling you they won't do business with you because you're not a member of the Better Business Bureau, trust me you don't need their business.

The only dealing I've ever had with the Better Business Bureau outside of them telling me they don't want my dirty porn money, is when a woman charged back her credit card.

Apparently this customer was so stupid that she charged back her credit card and still expected her purchase. Then we revoked access to her purchase automatically because that's what we do when people fuck us.

This woman was so stupid, that she complained to the Better Business Bureau about us. Even though we weren't members, the Better Business Bureau mediated between us and the stupid woman. When it was all said and done, the Better Business Bureau agreed with our claim against the woman because we provided all the relevant information.

However, this left a permanent record on their website with a complaint against us even though it was resolved. I just don't see the value in joining these organizations.

Maybe someone with a better experience can shed some light on this for me :) If so tweet me @bradgosse

# CHANGING THE RULES TO YOUR ADVANTAGE

# Chapter 29: Changing The Rules To Your Advantage

In order to be high functioning, it's often important to understand how social rules work and how to change them to your advantage. Some people get upset when I talk about things like this. Often because they have a victim's perspective. I don't believe anyone to be a victim when you change social rules. I'm going to lay out a few scenarios, some of them you may like and some you may dislike. My advice is to try them all yourself and see what happens. These are designed to help you get ahead in life and business.

**Jumping the dinner line.**
Have you ever gone out to dinner without reservations? A busy restaurant might tell you to wait 30 to 60 minutes for a table without reservations. The majority of people will sit down and begin waiting or find another place to eat without such a long line up. Personally, I don't like to wait in line for anything. Call me entitled. I don't care. I will walk up to the host or hostess with a folded $20 bill in my hand and quietly hand it to them asking if there's anything they can do to expedite things for us. I have never been denied a quick table using this method. 60 minutes of my time is worth far more than $20. And I know that that host or hostess isn't making very much per hour. In a nicer restaurant you might need a $50 bill or a $100 bill. But I don't eat at fancy places like that Mr. Rockefeller.

**Hotel suite upgrades.**
Most people don't realize how easy this is. Talk to most front desk clerks at hotels, you'd be surprised how few of them get

tips. When you arrive at a hotel you often tip the doorman for opening your door, a bell man for taking your bags, a waiter, cocktail waitress but never the front desk clerk. Now ask yourself this. Who has the most power over making your trip awesome or terrible at the moment you check-in? The front desk clerk. Most people walk up to the counter pull out their credit card and don't make eye contact with the front desk clerk. This is a fatal mistake. I prefer to walk up to the front desk clerk and shake their hand while they welcome me to their hotel. Inside my hand is a $20 or $50 bill depending on how nice the hotel is. The difference here is that a front desk clerk is not used to receiving a tip. Sometimes they will ask you what it's for. Simply say "that's for you" with a smile on your face. In my experience this has always gotten me a better room over the cheap one we reserve online.

**Jumping the retail line.**
This one really gets people going. Have you ever been at the grocery store, bookstore etc. where they have multiple lines? Of course you have. Everybody's been in the situation where you are the 5th or 6th person in line but the first person to notice a new checkout is opening. There are 2 types of people in this world. You have already decided who you are before continuing this paragraph. What do you do? Personally I like to take advantage of anything that saves me time. Without being aggressive, I will casually walk to the checkout counter that's just been opened. Usually taking the first position. Sometimes people can get mad, but no retail store that I know of has posted rules about how their lines work. Often I ignore people who get angry with me and they go away.

**Asking for forgiveness instead of permission.**

This is a pretty general rule for me. But whenever I'm looking to do something out of the ordinary, there are often questions about whether or not I'm breaking rules. These could be anybody's rules. In my experience, when breaking new ground and trying things nobody has tried before, asking for permission can throw a wrench into your machine before it even starts. Instead, charging ahead and getting things going seems to work better for me. People are often afraid of the unknown, and if you ask for permission to do things, they get scared. As a for instance, breaking my own rule, I contacted a well-known margarine company to see if they would be willing to allow my wife to print their name in her book as a recommended product. You wouldn't believe how difficult it was to not only reach the right person but to get a decision from them. In fact no decision was ever rendered. We printed the name in the book, and nobody complained. Execute your ideas, as long as you aren't breaking laws, you'll be fine.

**Ask questions with the outcome you desire.**
One of the easiest ways to spot a lack of confidence is when people ask questions from the negative. Someone might say to me: "I guess you wouldn't want to mail this to your list?". Well, now that you've made it extremely easy for me to say no. No. I don't want to mail this to my list. And thanks for making it easy.

Try saying this instead: "how can I help you get this out to your list?". Now you are asking from an assumptive position. You are assuming that I am going to mail it to my list. Your question involves facilitation. How you frame your questions often dictates the outcome. Change the way you ask and watch your success rate go through the roof.

Tell me how you change the rules yourself, hit me up on Twitter @bradgosse

# STOP WATCHING TV

# Chapter 30: Stop Watching TV

If you really want to get more done, giving up television is one of the most effective things you can do. Some of the most successful people I know don't watch the news. Many more don't watch television at all.

It's not the media's fault that bad news sells, it just does and they are in the business of selling the news. Or at least selling those bits of space in between the news. So if you know that the media is designed to scare the shit out of you, shouldn't you avoid it?

I still hear about relevant news, when I go to parties, dinners or just hang out with friends. But I only hear about the most important things that my friends and family think are relevant. To be honest I couldn't be bothered to hear about the rest. And it's so much more fun when people can tell you about something you don't know. It makes conversation more interesting.

My diet from the television tit started when my satellite service stopped working. My satellite dish is located about two thirds of the way up a 100 foot tower on my property. I had a feeling the satellite guy wouldn't be interested in climbing. I was right. Rather than pay my tower guys a ton of money I decided to cancel my satellite service. My wife and I had been using our Apple TV set-top box more and more, and so we thought we would try switching to download on-demand.

This way, we could still be entertained in our living room, but it would force us to make choices as opposed to settling for any old crap. Of course we never download the news, we only download seasons of TV shows and movies that interest us. The result is we spend much less time watching television and much more time interacting, playing Scrabble, video games, going out etc.

If you can't disconnect your television set you definitely can still go on a news diet. At the very least take 30 days away from the news and see if your life is any better. I can almost guarantee you'll have a better outlook at the end of 30 days. You owe it to yourself to try this. It's much easier than any diet in the real world.

Even morning news shows may seem innocent enough. But they constantly like to talk about the bad economy and how you can save money by clipping coupons or recycling fast food containers or some other bullshit. This is the worst way to start your day, thinking about clipping coupons. The problem with recessions is that the media loves them. They create stories around recession. I believe they perpetuate recessions and possibly even create them. A story about recession can start people on the path to not wanting to part with their money for fear there will be less to go around later. It becomes a vicious circle.

Like many of the things I recommend, this will come with much resistance. There are people especially in the baby boomer generation who believe that the news is essential to their lives. You will be accused of ignorance. Some people take great offense when others don't watch the news the way they do. They believe it's our job living in the first world to be aware of what's going on. I believe that unless you are willing to stand up for the wrongdoing in the world and try to change it, being aware of it doesn't make you a better person.

Some people don't even realize that the news media is a business. They actually see it as some kind of government service that delivers impartial stories. You don't need to argue with these people. It's best not to tell them about your news diet, they won't understand and it's not worth your energy to argue with them.

# DROPPING OUT OF SCHOOL

# Chapter 31: Dropping Out Of School

I think it's safe to say that the public school system is pretty much bankrupt.

Public-school was designed to prepare you for the factory floor. Repetitive learning, testing, bells, schedules, breaks, discipline, authority, conformity and losing the ability to think for yourself are all side effects of the current system. I believe that we now live in a world where information is at our disposal.

Just like the calculator made repetitive teaching like long division obsolete, our information age has made public education obsolete.

Think about it, home schooled kids score better on standardized tests than public schooled kids.

Here is a quote from John D Rockefeller's 1906 general education bulletin.

"In our dreams, people yield themselves with perfect docility to our molding hands. The present eduction conventions of intellectual and character education fade from their minds, and, unhampered by tradition, we work our own good will upon a grateful and responsive folk. We shall not try to make these people, or any of their children, into philosophers, or men of science. We have not to raise up from them authors, educators, poets or men of letters. We shall not search for great artists, painters, musicians nor lawyers, doctors, preachers, politicians, statesmen -- of whom we have an ample supply. The task is simple. We will organize children and teach them in a perfect way the things their fathers and mothers are doing in an imperfect way."

Long before any of us was born, people in positions of great power and wealth designed an education system to train their workers. I'm not going to get into conspiracy theories here, because I'm not sure they exist, but I do know that over 100 years ago several people influenced the way anyone learns in public school today.

If you are reading this, and you're considering dropping out of high school or skipping college, my advice is to do just that.

By the time you reach the 10th grade I believe you have learned all that public school has to offer. Now you have to unlearn much of what was taught in order to become a successful entrepreneur. The sooner you start this process, the better off you will be.

I believe that college and university have become prohibitively expensive for the average student. People are graduating with debt upwards of 6 figures. They then spend the next decade working for very little money while trying to pay off astronomical student loans. The system is broken, but people keep showing up, getting in line and becoming slaves to the bank before they even have income.

You don't need any pieces of paper or any kind of degree to own a business.

I dropped out of high school and people often ask me what I took in university. I remember once a woman asking me what I took in university because she wanted her son to follow a similar path to me. I was flattered, but when I told her that I was a high school dropout she was very surprised. I'm not saying this to brag (although it feels good to say out loud). I'm telling you this because you don't need a university education for people to think you are intelligent.

Of course there will always be the group of people who went to school and think that you aren't smart unless you went to college/university. Those people live in a bubble where they help each other climb the ladder in the corporate world. Most of them are too scared to stand on their own 2 feet and take the risks associated with entrepreneurship.

While my friends were studying hard, drinking hard, and getting high in college. I was attending the school of life. Learning to pay rent without help from my parents, having a day job while trying to build a business on the side, learning sales and marketing from the ground floor etc.

When they got out of school, all of that was just beginning for them. For me, I had a big head start. Fast forward to today. I make more money than just about anyone I can think of who went to school with me. Again not bragging (well maybe a little).

My only request is that you always maintain a thirst for knowledge. Long before the Internet came along, I would go to the public library and read up on subjects that interested me. I found that to be much more engaging than sitting in a classroom. Today if I want to learn how to do something, I'll download an e-book, video, MP3 or other media. The cool part is there are so many more people publishing content today, so I have lots of choice and can download a variety of materials from different experts and absorb it all.

Intelligence comes from within. It has much more to do with how well you learn, adapt and solve problems than it does with memorizing facts.

If you want to chat with me more about this hit me up on Twitter @bradgosse

# ACKNOWLEDGMENTS

# Acknowledgments

For some reason, this seems to be the hardest part of the entire book for me. First of all I don't know where to start and second I'm afraid I may miss somebody.

To my wife Claire. Thank you for your support and for believing in me even when it seemed impossible to win. You take care of everything for me and put up with my bullshit. I can't imagine life without you never mind how I could've written this book, or done anything functional in the last 15 years. I am very proud to call myself your husband. Many times, I have been working on this book while you happily make breakfast, lunch and dinner for me. Some days I would forget to eat if you weren't here with me to remind me to stop working. I look forward to more adventures and experiences with you.

Meg Schaefer. I can't even imagine what it's like to be my assistant. Between my cryptic messages and my ridiculous expectations I don't know how you put up with me. Without you, everything falls apart in my business. I hope this book and its success make everything a little bit more worth it for you :-) it's not always easy to work for me but I hope that the rewards have been worth it. Being able to count on you helps me to stay sane. You are my gatekeeper, webmaster, voice over artist, content creator, grunt worker, time manager, project manager, customer service representative and also a good friend. Claire and I were honored to be invited to your wedding this year. Thank you for including us :-)

To my joint venture partners in business. There are too many of you to name but I must mention a number of you. Anthony Aires, Ron Douglas, Evan Carmichael, E Brian Rose, Bryan Zimmerman, Paul Clifford, Dennis Becker, Rachel Rofe, Russell Ruffino, Andrew Lewin, Mark Lyford, Andy Fletcher, Maria Gudelis, Ted Payne, Alec Helmy, Simon Hodgkinson, Chris Ramsey, Holly Cotter, Jeremy Kelsall, Kevin Rogers, Mike Lewis, Mike Lantz, Tim Castleman, Justin Wheeler, David Walker, Willie Crawford, Mike Cowles, Dave Kosmayer, Charles Michael, Mark Hurson, Andrew Skelley, Kevin Riley, Sam England, Steve Benn, Steve Rosenbaum, Shane WIlliams, Seth Bias, Paul Klein, Stephen Renton, Colin Theriot (for helping with this book name and copy), Cindy Battye, Yanik Silver, Chris Munch, Brad Mitchell and the crew @ MojoHost.com my photographer Paul George and many more. Thank you for working with me and helping me get to where I am :-)

Justin Popovic. We met under hilarious circumstances and have become great friends and great business partners along the way. It's interesting how people can help each other grow. Thank you for helping me to realize my value as a public speaker and for motivating me to become one. Working with you is always easy because you have a very strong work ethic. I appreciate our friendship and partnerships more than you will know.

Cherry Tanoy, my cartoonist. Every drawing in this book is thanks to your talent. I was very lucky to find you. Thank you for giving me artwork I can be proud of. I remember when you told me that drawing cartoons for me was the perfect job because it never felt like work. That's the best compliment I could receive. I'm so glad you enjoy what you do. We are very happy to have you on our team.

Jennifer Wozniak. You are still fairly new to my company but your work makes life easier for all of us. It's funny to think that we started out as pen-pals when we were teenagers. Then, found each other on social media and began chatting again. Before I knew it you were part of my team. Your contribution is extremely valuable and I appreciate everything you bring to the table.

To all my coaching clients. I won't single any of you out. But many of you helped me to figure out the chapters for this book. You know who you are. It's likely that I ran off and shot a YouTube video minutes after our coaching call to rant about something we discussed. Now it's a chapter of my book. Hopefully the lessons I have taught you have been beneficial. Each of you has also taught me your own lessons which I will carry with me through life. Many of those lessons made it to this book. So thank you for that.

To my mother. Thank you for raising me differently. When I would go to school and have trouble with authority, often I would come home with a letter and usually some kind of punishment. I'm sure other parents lost it under similar circumstances. You allowed me to resist authority at a very young age. I'm not sure I'd even be writing this book today if it weren't for that kind of liberal parenting. You also taught me to see things differently. Lastly, you taught me how to communicate effectively by ensuring that my grammar was impeccable. Even when I was surrounded by special ed kids. You made sure to correct me every time I slipped. I may not have liked it then, but it's the reason why people often expect that I am university educated and are shocked to find out that I dropped out of high school.

To my father. The lessons I got from you were learned later in life. Working for you gave me a crash course in business ownership and entrepreneurship that I couldn't have gotten anywhere else. More importantly, you taught me to stand up for myself and to never take shit from people. You are the first person I witnessed firing a customer. The experience was borderline frightening the first time it happened. But I quickly learned there was a method to your madness. I will never look back. You also taught me how to sell. I believe salesmanship is part nature and part nurture. I think I got both parts from you.

To my closest friends. Dave and Aileen, Maggy and Dave, Justin and Jessica. I don't maintain a large number of close friends, and I know that most of you don't either, so thank you for choosing me to be among that group. Each of you is my friend because of your awesomeness. Thank you for your ongoing support and for always being in my corner. It's great to have you rooting for me. I hope that I am as good a friend to you as you are to me.

There are very few people who I would consider mentors or people I look up to. Here is a short list of the people who have influenced me and this book. Scott Stratten, Amber Mac, Rajesh Setty, Seth Godin, Timothy Ferris, Kevin Rose, Malcolm Gladwell, Abbie Hoffman, Hunter S. Thompson, Gary Vaynerchuk, Tucker Max, Donny Deutsch, Keith Ferrazzi, and Anthony Robbins.

To you my customer. Thank you for purchasing this book, and anything else you may buy from me now or in the future. I hope that I deliver more value to you than the dollars you put in my pocket. Thank you for allowing me to live the lifestyle I enjoy while I deliver products to you :-)

I'm absolutely sure I have missed people. If I missed you please accept my apologies.

If you want to connect with me there are a few ways to do it. I would love to hear your thoughts on this book.

Website: http://chronicmarketer.com
Twitter: @bradgosse
Email: newsletter@chronicmarketer.com
Facebook: http://gopo.me/chronicfb

If you want me to speak at your event or if you want to work with me in another capacity, email my assistant megan@yourbrainmedia.com

Made in the USA
Lexington, KY
20 April 2012